IMAGES
of America

BOSTON'S THEATER DISTRICT

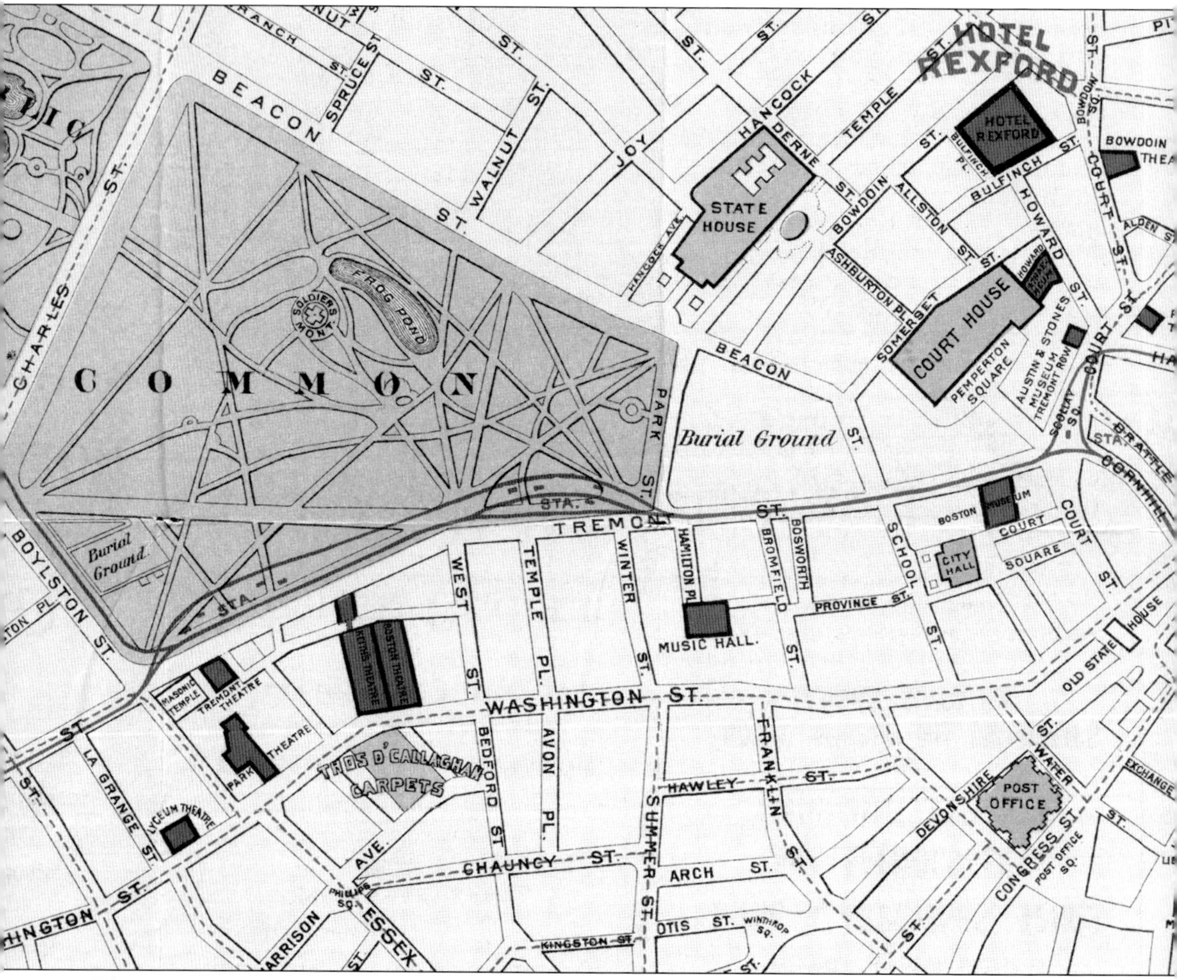

This tourist map from 1899 shows the burgeoning theater district and the newly constructed subway that ran beneath Boston Common. Another 24 theaters and concert halls were built in Boston between 1900 and 1935. Thirteen of them sprouted up along this half-mile stretch of Washington and Tremont Streets that had a long history as a commercial crossroads. To the north lay Scollay Square, teeming with temptations of its own. (Courtesy of Boston Public Library.)

On the Cover: In 1917, Harry Houdini escaped from a straitjacket while dangling upside down 100 feet in the air from Keith's Theatre. The Tremont Street entrance led through the Crystal Tunnel from Boston Common to Washington Street, where B.F. Keith, the father of vaudeville, ran three theaters with combined seating for 6,000 people. A sign atop the Majestic Theatre, built in 1903, is visible in the distance. (Courtesy of Library of Congress.)

IMAGES
of America

BOSTON'S THEATER DISTRICT

Dale Stinchcomb

ARCADIA
PUBLISHING

Copyright © 2021 by Dale Stinchcomb
ISBN 978-1-4671-0589-7

Published by Arcadia Publishing
Charleston, South Carolina

Printed in the United States of America

Library of Congress Control Number: 2020937986

For all general information, please contact Arcadia Publishing:
Telephone 843-853-2070
Fax 843-853-0044
E-mail sales@arcadiapublishing.com
For customer service and orders:
Toll-Free 1-888-313-2665

Visit us on the Internet at www.arcadiapublishing.com

To my friend and colleague Peter X. Accardo.

Contents

Acknowledgments

As a curator myself, I take considerable pride in acknowledging the curators and archivists who contributed time and expertise to this book. Many did so in the midst of the coronavirus pandemic, which made their assistance even more crucial than usual. I would especially like to thank David Leopold of the Al Hirschfeld Foundation, Crista Dix of the Griffin Museum of Photography, Donna Russo of Historic New England, Andrew Elder of The History Project, Claire Blechman of the Peabody Essex Museum, Andrew Ku of Playbill Inc., Nicole McAllister of Revolutionary Spaces, Julia Howington of Suffolk University, and Kyle Boyd of UMass Amherst Libraries. I am equally grateful to Phil Boucher, Marc J. Franklin, Spencer Grant, Bruce T. Martin, and Zach Pagano as well as the Jerry Berndt Estate, Emerson Colonial Theatre, the Leslie R. Jones family, and John Toto for making their photographs available for our enjoyment.

I owe a deep debt of gratitude to my colleagues at Harvard and the Houghton Library, particularly Mary Haegert, Thomas Lingner, Matthew Wittmann, and Robert Zinck. Generous support from the Houghton Library director, Tom Hyry, in the form a Katharine F. Pantzer Jr. Staff Research Fellowship, enabled me to cast a wide net for photographs. Peter X. Accardo, Andrea Cawelti, Christine Jacobson, Irina Klyagin, Mitch Nakaue, and Susan Radovsky listened graciously as I tested out material.

Iris Fanger, Felicia Shapiro, Dennis Stinchcomb, and William P. Stoneman have been an unfailing source of advice and encouragement. Without the patience and insight of my editor Caitrin Cunningham, this project would not have been possible.

I have benefited from a number of sources, namely Donald C. King's *The Theatres of Boston* (2005), which is a gold mine of tidbit facts. This book cannot hope—and does not pretend—to be as exhaustive. I turned more than once to Elliot Norton's *Broadway Down East* (1978) and to David S. Shields's website Broadway Photographs. An unpublished guide to the theater district by Fredric Woodbridge Wilson also enriched this book by taking me down paths I had not anticipated.

Introduction

Boston's love-hate affair with the theater goes back centuries. The first public performance for which we have a record took place in 1750 at a coffeehouse on State Street. The play's success brought swift condemnation. As citizens crowded the doorway in hopes of getting a closer look, a near-riot broke out. Zealous legislators responded by making it a crime to sponsor, perform, or even attend a play. Such amusements were frivolous, they reasoned, and tended to increase "immorality, impiety and contempt of religion." Little did they suspect that their city on a hill would one day harbor the largest concentration of playhouses outside of Manhattan.

Some converts to the theater still dared to put on plays. In the early 1790s, the Concert Hall and the New Exhibition Room, theaters in all but name, offered the perfect cover. There, plays were "exhibited" or "delivered"—but never "performed"—usually under the thin guise of "moral lectures." It is worth pointing out that the act of smuggling theaters inside museums persisted throughout the 19th century, a telling sign that some Bostonians were not yet comfortable with the idea; nor were they likely to be in the future.

There were other obvious hypocrisies. While actors struggled for respectability among the city's Puritan descendants, Charlotte Cushman emerged as America's first international stage star and a much beloved citizen. More than a century later, the stage continued to be censored more vigorously and with greater moral conviction than anywhere else in the nation. Yet despite their vigilance, city officials reluctantly carved out a piece of the theater district in the 1970s, designating it for strip clubs, pornographic cinemas, and other adult entertainments. The existence of the infamous Combat Zone seemed to fulfill old Puritan fears that the stage would corrupt public morals.

These incongruities are part of what make Boston's theater district so compelling. Its own history began two years after the ban on theaters was lifted. In 1796, a crude playhouse was built on the edge of Boston Common, on the present site of a multiplex cinema. It soon floundered, failing to draw patrons away from the more centrally located Boston Theatre, then the only game in town. The Great Fire of 1872 reshaped the urban landscape, and more theaters grew up alongside retail shops and warehouses on Washington Street. A thriving piano trade moved into Boylston and Tremont Streets, where decades earlier the Haymarket Theatre had gone belly up. Boston's appetite for music spurred the construction of larger, more lavish venues for opera and musical theater. And by 1930, the area had evolved into a vibrant bohemia of burlesque halls and movie palaces, vaudeville houses, and regal stages. In its heyday, most of the city's playhouses were within a half-mile radius of Washington and Tremont Streets, bounded by Scollay Square to the north and Chinatown to the south. Like much of old Boston, the strip was easily walkable and passed through the commercial center of present-day Downtown Crossing. It was also conveniently close to the Beacon Hill residences of Boston's elite patrons of the arts.

More than any other figure, Clarence Blackall shaped the visual experience of the theater district. Blackall was a graduate of the École des Beaux-Arts in Paris and one of the most prolific theater architects of his day. He is credited with designing some 22 Boston theaters and upwards of

300 theaters nationwide. His finest work survives intact at the Colonial, his masterpiece, and the intimate Wilbur, the monumental Wang (formerly the Metropolitan), and in the elegant facade of the Modern. These theaters are showplaces in every sense, places to see and be seen—an offer that Boston high society seldom refused. For the many working-class families who flocked to the district, an evening at the theater was as close to the baroque splendors of Europe as they were likely to get, which is why so many of Blackall's designs borrowed freely from sites that loomed large in the public imagination: the Hall of Mirrors and the Grand Trianon at Versailles, the Paris Opera House, Pompeii, Florence, Venice, and Rome. Only the Wilbur was designed in the Federal Revival style that nodded to the town's colonial past.

For much of the 20th century, attending the theater carried with it a special thrill—a responsibility even. Shows bound for Broadway previewed at the Shubert, Colonial, and Wilbur Theatres, giving audiences a firsthand look at new work, warts and all. The fact that Bostonians saw the shows before their New York neighbors was a point of pride. And producers looked to local audiences and critics to gauge a success or failure. For those old enough to remember, Broadway previews rank among their fondest memories of the theater district.

Of the approximately 50 theaters built in Boston over the last 200 years, well over half have been torn down. All but four of Blackall's buildings were demolished. As a result, the theater district has shrunk considerably. Scant traces remain of the Combat Zone that once threatened to overrun the area. Its sleaze was largely expunged in 1990s, leaving a row of vacant, crumbling theaters in its wake.

Today, the theater district is back in the limelight. Most of the surviving venues have undergone historic transformations at great cost and commitment. Their rebirth has attracted a new generation of playgoers as well as new investment to downtown Boston. Luxury high-rises are going up on Washington Street. And an influx of developers has begun rebranding the surrounding area as the Ladder District, referring to the narrow side streets that connect Washington and Tremont like rungs on a ladder. The soon-to-be trendy neighborhood may be a shadow of its former self, but its survival is nothing short of miraculous. Luckily for us, the magnificent theaters are not encased in amber but are back at the center of Boston's thriving performing arts community.

One

Out of the Ashes

To say that theaters were fire-prone would be the understatement of the 19th century. Some 460 fires plagued theaters across America and Europe between 1800 and 1877. One British engineer calculated the average lifespan of a theater in the United States at just 13 years. Fire and the threat of fire had an equally profound impact on the Boston stage. The city's first public playhouse burned down within four years; a nearby theater caught fire within four months. The latter was rebuilt, only to burn three more times over the next 50 years.

The effects of fire were often felt indirectly. When the Great Fire of 1872 decimated the central business district, the theaters along its western boundary were spared. On its heels came a period of rapid rebuilding that transformed lower Washington Street into a vibrant center of manufacturing and commerce. The population boomed, and a rialto was born.

In 1882, Thomas Edison's incandescent light bulb greatly reduced theater mortality rates in the new district. The Bijou became the first theater outfitted throughout with electricity. (It had 13 exits for added insurance.) Most theaters adopted electricity slowly, in combination with gas, meaning the old hazards remained. Fire would continue to shape the district well into the 20th century. Ironically, it was stricter fire codes brought about by the horrific Cocoanut Grove fire in 1942 that hastened the Bijou's demise. Egress became a watchword, and consequently some of the city's oldest theaters were demolished.

On a practical note, the many conflagrations led to an increase of new theaters with old names. For example, Boston has had three Tremont Theatres, three Boston Theatres, three Globe Theatres, and three Gaiety Theatres, just to name a few. Not all were rebuilt in the same location, so the name game can get confusing.

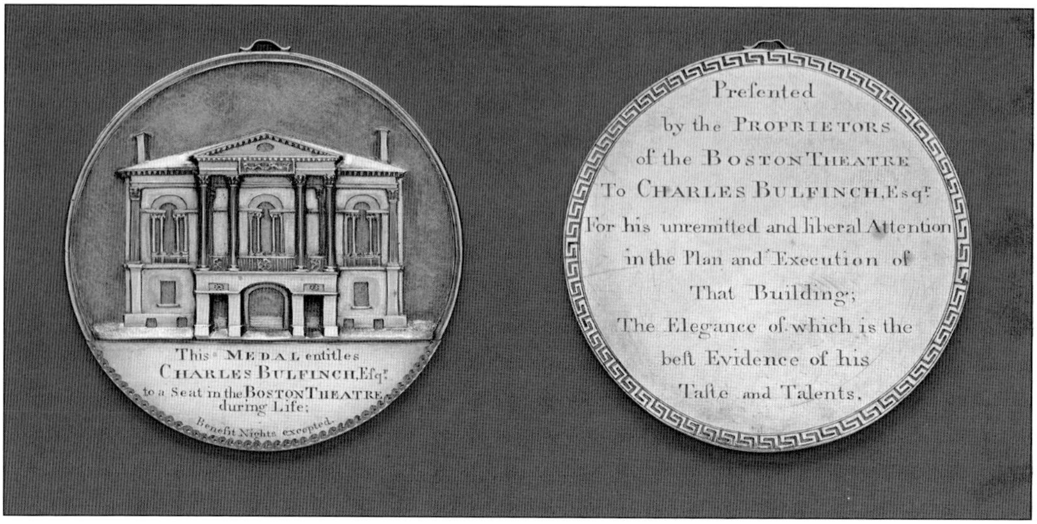

"New Theatre opened this Day," John Quincy Adams recorded dryly in his diary on February 3, 1794. Adams had lobbied to overturn the 1750 ban on theatrical entertainments and then invested in the city's first theater. The cost was double the original estimate of $40,000. But the proprietors were so gratified with their new theater that they presented architect Charles Bulfinch with the gold medal above entitling him to a seat for life, "Benefit Nights excepted." The honor was short-lived, for the building at Federal and Franklin Streets caught fire four years later. Below, an allegorical scene depicts the burning. In the foreground, the goddess Athena holds a scroll showing the simpler facade of the hastily rebuilt theater, above which a phoenix rises. (Above, courtesy of Harvard Theatre Collection; below, courtesy of Revolutionary Spaces.)

The wealthiest patrons arrived by carriage, alighting under the porte cochere. Attendants escorted them to their boxes through a grand lobby with adjoining parlors for tea and cards. Separate side entrances led to cheaper seats in the pit and gallery and also kept social classes from mingling. The playhouse was torn down in 1852, just as plans for a second, grander Boston Theatre were underway. (Courtesy of Harvard Theatre Collection.)

In 1796, a competing playhouse opened opposite Boston Common. The tall, wood frame structure (in rear) looked more like a barn than a theater. But what the Haymarket Theatre lacked in refinements, it made up for in size. It flourished for a time, but demand fell sharply when the Boston Theatre reopened. Fire-wary neighbors purchased the property in 1803, aided by the Haymarket's rivals, and had it razed. (Courtesy of Boston Public Library.)

Fire-and-brimstone Baptists bought the struggling Tremont Theatre (right) in 1843 and closed it down. Even after its dedication as Tremont Temple, the hall continued to be rented out for secular events. It was plagued by fire and rebuilt four times. The architect Isaiah Rogers also designed Tremont House across the street. (Courtesy of Boston Public Library.)

The present Tremont Temple was built with a first-class theater in mind by Clarence Blackall. His 1896 design called for folding seats instead of pews. For decades, the house of worship led a double life as a cinema. Lighting fixtures inspired by the Blue Mosque in Istanbul float beneath the shimmering white and gold ceiling like a sea of jellyfish. (Photograph by Frank Cousins; courtesy of Boston Public Library.)

The reverse was true of the Howard Athenaeum, which looked more like a temple than a theater. Four months after opening in 1844, a fireball effect during a performance of *Pizarro* ignited the scenery and burned the former tabernacle to the ground. It was rebuilt in Quincy granite by Isaiah Rogers, retaining its church-like appearance, pictured here in the 1850s. (Courtesy of Boston Public Library.)

The National Theatre put down roots in the West End well before playhouses began to cluster downtown. The site on Portland Street was originally used for equestrian performances, but in 1832, a new owner erected a proscenium stage. Two decades later, an early-morning blaze incinerated the building, leaving behind only an iron safe. (Courtesy of Boston Public Library.)

Broadsides posted outside the entrance to the rebuilt theater date this photograph to 1860. The National carved out a niche for itself by restaging popular melodramas like the one advertised here. *Rob Roy* played continuously at the Boston Museum from 1848 through the 1870s. Clearly, the National wanted a piece of the action. As managers came and went, so did the theater's names. Willard's National Theatre changed to People's National Theatre, then to Union Concert Hall. The theater met a familiar end, burning in 1863. (Courtesy of Harvard Theatre Collection.)

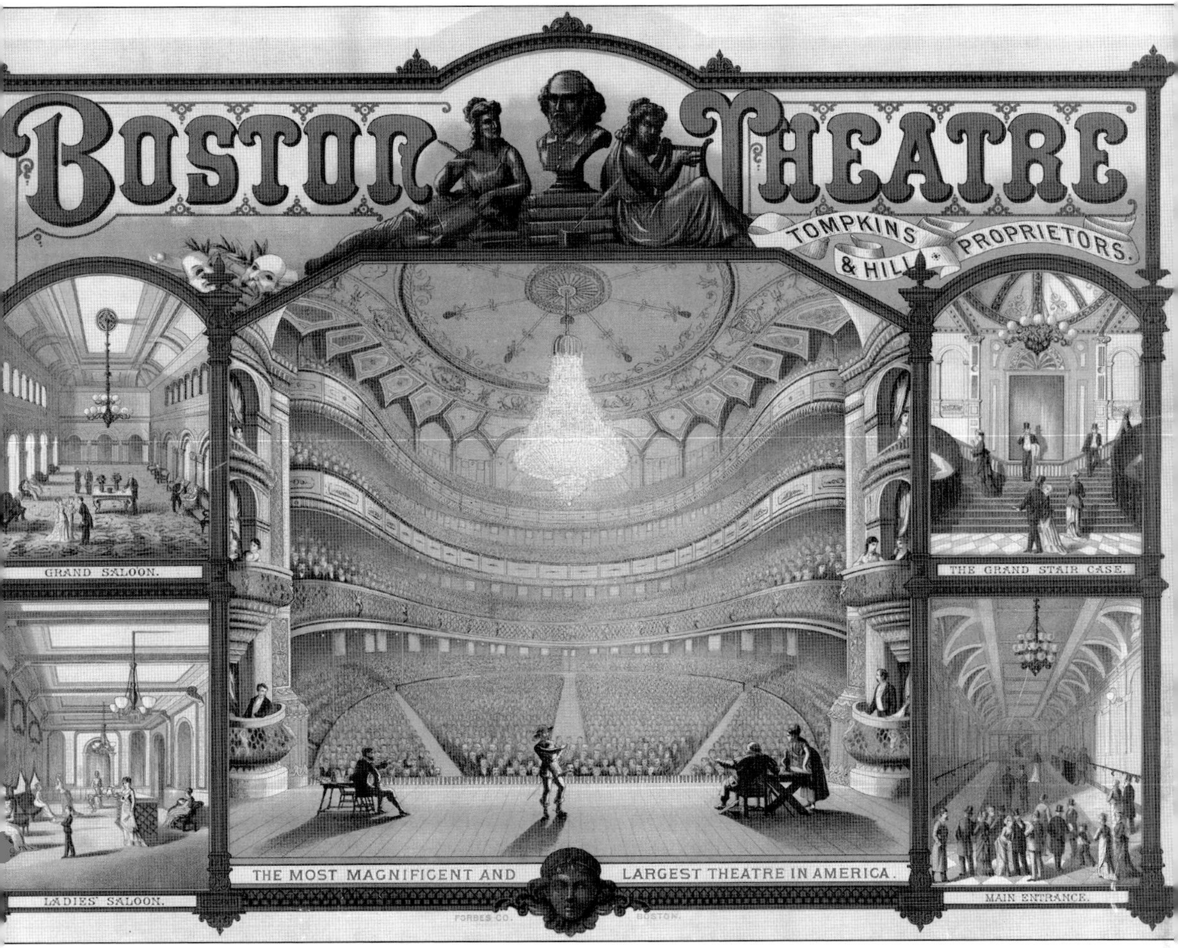

A new Boston Theatre eclipsed the old in 1854. This lively poster, printed by the Forbes Company, which specialized in theatrical playbills and advertisements, depicts the cavernous auditorium surrounded by three balconies: the dress circle, the family circle, and the gallery. At center hangs an enormous chandelier with hundreds of gas burners that took half an hour to light. On opening night, one critic praised his seat above all else, "being so ingeniously contrived as to fold up and allow passing." The theater's managers claimed, perhaps falsely, that these were the first folding chairs ever used in a theater. Playgoing was a social occasion, and the four vignettes capture the excitement of an evening at the theater. Still, seating was segregated. A notice printed in an early program announced that "a box in the second tier has been assigned to colored persons, who can only be admitted to that part of the house." (Courtesy of Harvard Theatre Collection.)

By the mid-19th century, Washington Street was a bustling thoroughfare connecting the city, then situated at the end of a peninsula, to the mainland. A narrow wooden entrance made to look like stone belied the true size and grandeur of the new Boston Theatre. It was the largest playhouse in the country, far surpassing the 2,000-seat Music Hall built two years earlier. (Courtesy of Boston Public Library.)

The Great Fire of 1872 laid waste to a 65-acre swath of downtown, consuming 776 buildings in its path. The blaze was extinguished just short of the historic Old South Meeting House, whose silhouette is visible in the background. The fire spared businesses on the northwest side of Washington Street while destroying others on the opposite side. The theaters to the south were unscathed. (Courtesy of Boston Public Library.)

Another fire six months later destroyed the Globe Theatre and over 100 buildings on the surrounding blocks. Several of the affected businesses had been uprooted by the Great Fire of 1872 the previous November. The inferno took place on Memorial Day, while most establishments were closed, and therefore attracted a great many onlookers. Note the steam-powered engines, an early method of fighting fire with fire. Luckily, the Globe was insured, along with its stock of scenery and costumes. The rest of the season's bookings moved across the street to the Park Theatre. A second Globe reopened on the same site the following year but burned again in 1894. (Courtesy of Harvard Theatre Collection.)

After the Great Fire of 1872, city planners seized the opportunity to straighten crooked streets. Washington Street was extended to the north and the buildings renumbered. As a result, the Globe was given a new address. This pre-fire photograph shows the earlier number. Charlotte Cushman gave her farewell performance at the second Globe in 1875, and Sarah Bernhardt made her Boston debut there in 1880. (Courtesy of Revolutionary Spaces.)

The resurrected Globe was larger and more lavish than its predecessor, as evidenced by the ornate box office. Tickets to performances by the Boston Ideal Opera Company in 1884 ranged from 25¢ to $12. An offshoot of the Ideals toured extensively as the Bostonians and was hailed by critics as the country's foremost comic opera troupe. (Courtesy of Harvard Theatre Collection.)

Fire damaged the Great Hall at the Boston Museum in 1899. The museum-theater combo had been in decline for years after the death of its founder Moses Kimball and the disbanding of its celebrated stock company. The collections of fine art and natural history specimens were dispersed. The painting of George Washington by Thomas Sully, which hangs on the far wall, is now safely preserved in the Museum of Fine Arts in Boston. After half a century, the museum on Tremont Street was torn down and replaced by an office block bearing Kimball's name. (Photograph by N.L. Stebbins; courtesy of Harvard Theatre Collection.)

In 1882, the Bijou Theatre became the first fully electrified playhouse in America. Thomas Edison himself supervised the installation of 644 incandescent bulbs throughout the house. In place of footlights, an arc of 190 electric lamps illuminated the stage from behind the horseshoe-shaped proscenium. Lighted sets for the premiere of Gilbert and Sullivan's *Iolanthe* left the audience in a daze of wonder: "Never have we seen a steadier and softer light in a theatre," the *Boston Globe* reported. The theater's sumptuous interior boasted a Moorish ceiling and chandeliers left over from an order for the Khedive of Egypt. Today, a spartan facade on Washington Street between the Citizens Bank Opera House and the Emerson Paramount Center is all that remains of the Bijou's former opulence. (Courtesy of Harvard Theatre Collection.)

A single Edison bulb survives from the Bijou, stored away for years, far from bumping elbows. While electric light was softer and safer than gas, it presented fresh challenges for actors. "The effect was like that of a dozen [spotlights] shining directly into one's eyes," complained one Bijou actor. "For weeks I saw that gleaming little wire constantly before me." (Courtesy of Harvard Theatre Collection.)

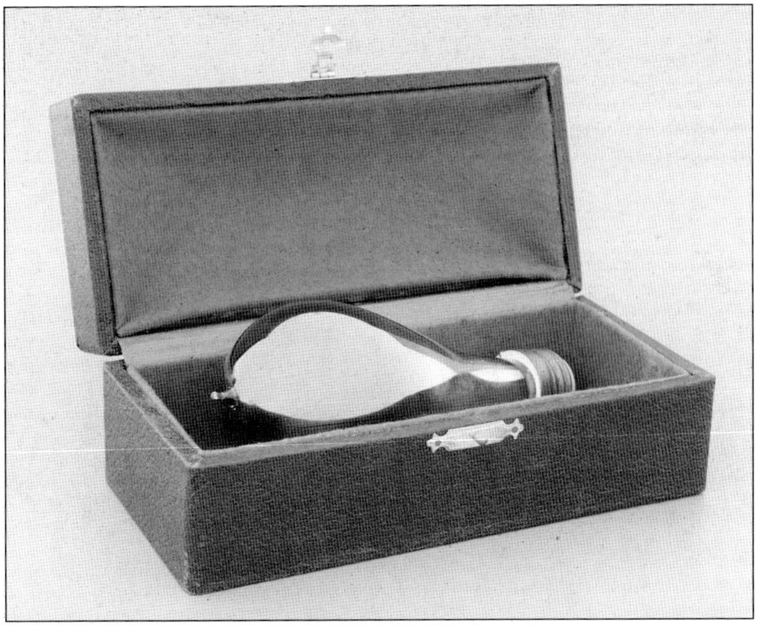

Before electricity, virtually all dramatic photographs were restaged in a studio using props and backcloths hauled there by the actors. Mid-action shots were impossible in the dim light of gas lamps, making this image a very early record of a live performance. Note the music stands peeping above the Bijou stage. (Photograph by N.L. Stebbins; courtesy of Harvard Theatre Collection.)

In 1885, Boston photographer Charles F. Conly successfully used electric light to photograph the audience at the Bijou Theatre. Though Conly used an "instantaneous" process, he had a tough time getting the audience to keep still for the five seconds needed for exposure. Reporters picked up on his irritation: "Ladies who were perfectly satisfied with their personal appearance before now began to find some fault in their wardrobe which required immediate attention. The gentlemen threw back their overcoats that the silk linings might have a respectable representation in the camera and struck various unnatural and uncomfortable attitudes supposed to be picturesque." It took three tries to get a satisfactory image. Copies were distributed as souvenirs at the end of the night. This photograph must have been a trial shot, taken as the audience filtered in. (Courtesy of Harvard Theatre Collection.)

Cocoanut Grove, on the edge of the theater district, was the scene of the deadliest nightclub fire in US history. On November 28, 1942, an inferno trapped hundreds of panicked revelers as they jammed the club's single revolving door. The other exits had been bolted shut to prevent patrons from leaving without paying. Nearly 500 perished within minutes. (Courtesy of Boston Public Library.)

When an electrical fire destroyed the set for *Golda*, the production was forced across the street to the Shubert Theatre, resulting in two identical marquees for its star Anne Bancroft. The stripped-down version enraptured audiences in Boston but stumbled when it arrived on Broadway in full dress. It closed after nine weeks, forfeiting its entire investment. (Courtesy of the Bettmann Archive via Getty Images.)

After Cocoanut Grove, Boston's oldest theaters were troubled less by the threat of fire than by demolition. It would take a combination of the two to topple the Old Howard. On June 20, 1961, firefighters battled a three-alarm blaze that swept through the century-old landmark. The infamous burlesque house had been slated for demolition by the Boston Redevelopment Authority, even as a campaign was underway to save it. That same day, the city ordered a wrecking crew to pull down what was left of the stone structure. The Boston Fire Department concluded that the fire was "of undetermined origin." But many fans suspected foul play, seeing as how the fire cleared the way for the $100 million development of Government Center. (Photograph by Charles Frani; courtesy of the West End Museum.)

Two

PIANO ROW

The piano industry was big business in Boston. The city had been at the forefront of the fledgling piano trade since Jonas Chickering hung out his shingle on Common Street (later Tremont) in 1823. Chickering was an innovator, and the pianos that bore his name had a reputation for superb craftsmanship and design. Before long, Chickering and his competitors overtook their European rivals, and the center of piano manufacturing shifted decisively to American soil. In 1896, the five largest piano makers in the world were American, and more than half of the world's pianos were made domestically, many of them by immigrant craftsmen in Boston and the surrounding towns.

By 1891, three-quarters of the city's 34 dealers had set up shop along a two-block stretch of Boylston and Tremont Streets known as "Piano Row." Few of the firms still carry cachet in the rarefied world of piano manufacture: Steinert, Vose, Jewett, Wurlitzer, Starck, Emerson, Mason & Hamlin, Ivers & Pond, and of course Chickering. They were joined by organ retailers and music publishers like Etsey and Oliver Ditson, whose 10-story office building still stands at 178–179 Tremont Street. So dense was the concentration that an 1895 guidebook listed Piano Row as the "headquarters of the musical profession."

The construction in 1852 of Boston's first temple to the performing arts, blandly named the Music Hall, fueled the city's musical ambitions. Other grand edifices followed, including three on Piano Row: Steinert Hall and the Colonial and Majestic Theatres. Initially designed for opera, the Majestic's stage was quickly usurped by a new mode of entertainment: motion pictures. Buffeted by a series of near-mortal blows from the phonograph and the radio, the piano industry faded too. Today, M. Steinert & Sons is the last stalwart of Piano Row, which was designated a national historic landmark in 1980. Its buried gem of a concert hall has received renewed attention of late, and there is reason to hope that it might one day be filled again with music.

A boring brick exterior hides one of Boston's oldest auditoriums. The Music Hall sits in the center of a city block, accessible by two alleyways off Tremont and Winter Streets. With no facade to fuss over, architect George Snell dispensed with ornament altogether. Henry James described the pedestrian approach from Hamilton Place, shown here in 1896, as "expectant and ominous." (Courtesy of Harvard Theatre Collection.)

The Music Hall is more than a monument to Yankee thrift. It is a cultural landmark. From 1852 until the end of the century, it was the city's premiere concert venue. It also hosted lectures by abolitionists and literary lights. Oscar Wilde visited in 1882. The space was used for civic celebrations as well, decked out here for Independence Day in 1876. (Courtesy of Boston Public Library.)

A 5,474-pipe organ was unveiled to much fanfare in November 1863. The behemoth fit snugly under the Music Hall's 65-foot ceiling. It was the first concert organ in the Americas—no mean feat when one considers that musical instruments of any kind were strictly forbidden in Puritan meetinghouses. An equally imposing statue of Beethoven by Thomas Crawford stood at its feet, peering out into the crowd. (Courtesy of Boston Public Library.)

The Great Organ was evicted in 1884 to clear the platform for the Boston Symphony Orchestra, which had purchased a controlling interest in the hall ahead of its first concert in 1881. A sounding board was installed in its place to amplify the orchestra. Repeated remodelings have gutted the Victorian interior, and no trace remains of the lofty vaults and overhanging balconies. (Photograph by A.H. Rickards; courtesy of Historic New England.)

Patrons line up on Winter Place for tickets to the Boston Symphony Orchestra. When the Music Hall was threatened with demolition in the late 1890s, the orchestra decamped to a permanent home on the wild frontier of Huntington Avenue. An exodus of the finer arts followed in its wake, and new stages sprung up on reclaimed land in Boston's Back Bay. Chickering Hall left Tremont Street in 1901, and the New England Conservatory, an early tenant of the Music Hall and the country's first college of music, moved to Jordan Hall in 1903, joined by the Boston Opera House and the Museum of Fine Arts in 1909. Thereafter, the Music Hall slipped in stature, and new venues along Piano Row rose up to fill the void. The Music Hall's organ survives in a hall specially built for it in Methuen, Massachusetts. (Courtesy of Boston Symphony Orchestra Archives.)

In 1810, Boylston Hall opened above the market at the comer of Washington and Boylston Streets. It was designed by Charles Bulfinch, the architect of the first Boston Theatre and the Massachusetts State House. The Handel and Haydn Society, formed in 1815, occasionally gave concerts there. The august ensemble is still around, but the market is long gone, replaced in 1887 by a larger structure. This 1870s view looks west on Boylston Street toward the intersection with Tremont Street and Piano Row. Playbills for the Boston, Globe, and Park Theatres are barely visible on the outside wall. (Photograph by D.W. Butterfield; courtesy of Boston Public Library.)

Interior views of 19th-century music shops are rare. This wood engraving appeared on the cover of an 1853 catalog from Richardson's Musical Exchange, a Boston retailer that specialized in foreign and American sheet music and books on music. The company also bought and sold secondhand pianos. One instrument is visible at the far end of the store, past the rows of filing cabinets. (Courtesy of Harvard Theatre Collection.)

In the 1890s, Ivers & Pond relocated its showroom to the ground floor of the Masonic Temple, the second lodge to be built at the busy corner of Boylston and Tremont Streets. On the far left, Everett Pianos has splashed its name across the side of the building at 180 Tremont Street. (Photograph by Moulton-Erickson; courtesy of Boston Public Library.)

Boylston station is the self-proclaimed gateway to the theater district. Though underwhelming today, it was a subject of intense fascination and pride in 1897. Some citizens did complain that the stone headhouses resembled mausoleums. Along Tremont Street, Etsey supplied organs to a ballooning number of movie houses, and the Tremont Theatre (with flagpole at center) stands on the site of the district's earliest playhouse, the Haymarket. (Photograph by T.E. Marr; courtesy of Boston Public Library.)

The nation's first subway was the 19th-century version of the Big Dig. The initial .6-mile segment, now part of the Green Line, ran underneath the Boston Common from Boylston Street to Park Street, along part of Piano Row. Not much has changed at Boylston station since opening day, September 1, 1897. Although back then, the tunnel walls and steelwork were neatly whitewashed. (Courtesy of City of Boston Archives.)

Residents of the Hotel Pelham (left) huddle at their windows as a circus parade winds its way up Boylston Street along Piano Row. Constructed in 1857, the Hotel Pelham was the first apartment building of its kind on the eastern seaboard. "French flats," like the Pelham and the Hotel Boylston, replaced the ubiquitous brick rowhouse as Boston grew from a provincial town of 30,000 in 1800

to a city of a quarter million in 1870. Next door, the Colonial Building (and Theatre) rises from the original site of the Boston Public Library, which relocated to Copley Square in 1895. In its absence, an actual zoo moved in, and the former reading room was pressed into service as a music hall aptly named Sans Souci or "carefree." (Courtesy of Boston Public Library.)

The Colonial Theatre is hidden inside a no-frills office building perched on the edge of Boston Common. It opened in December 1900 with a sold-out production of *Ben Hur*. Demand for tickets was so great that some waited at the box office for over 40 hours. Those with means hired strangers to stand in line for them. The show's much-touted scene featured a live chariot race with eight horses galloping on treadmills. Note the original marquee. As was customary for the time, the main lobby was off-limits to patrons in cheaper seats. A separate entry on the left provided access to the gallery, just as it had been at Boston's first theater. (Photograph by T.E. Marr; courtesy of Boston Public Library.)

As wealthy residents withdrew to new mansions in the Back Bay, their posh dwellings gave way to offices and piano showrooms. The change was driven in part by the southward expansion of the commercial district after the Great Fire of 1872. This photograph offers a placid view down Boylston Street, shortly after the opening of the Colonial Theatre. Construction has shifted down the street, near the entrance to Boylston Place. (Courtesy of Boston Public Library.)

More circus elephants parade through Park Square at the western end of Piano Row. Selwyn's Park Square Theatre (top left) was another of Clarence Blackall's creations, opening in 1914. It yielded to a parking garage in the 1920s. Overhead, a web of electrified streetcar cables crisscrosses the square. (Photograph by Leslie Jones; courtesy of Boston Public Library.)

The Little Building has anchored the corner of Tremont and Boylston Streets since 1917, when it supplanted the Hotel Pelham. Developers dubbed it the "City Under One Roof" for its novel mix of retail and office space. At ground level, a two-story arcade created an interior street complete with its own subway entrance, post office, restaurants, and basement automat. Among its tenants was a centralized ticketing office for all Shubert-run theaters. A network of corridors linked the Boylston Street subway station to underground lobbies at the neighboring Majestic and Plymouth Theatres. Though extant, the passageways have since been sealed off. (Photograph by L.H. Abdalian; courtesy of Boston Public Library.)

The monumental Majestic Theatre is the focal point of Piano Row. Its architect, John Galen Howard, trained in Paris and brought Beaux-Arts principles to bear on his only Boston building. Classical references abound but are interpreted with a modern flair. Hundreds of electric bulbs line the carved (and fireproof) terra-cotta arches, mounted in rosettes and behind the stained-glass windows. The alleyway on the right used to be Van Rensselaer Place. It was renamed Allen's Alley after comedian Fred Allen, whose popular radio show featured a fictional back street with the same name. Allen, a Boston native, often used the alley to reach the stage door of the Majestic. The Plymouth and Colonial Theatres also had stage doors that opened onto the alley, making it a natural spot for fans to congregate. The Majestic Theatre was a gift to the citizens of Boston from Eben Dyer Jordan, the scion of retail giant Jordan Marsh. Jordan also funded the construction of the first Boston Opera House and Jordan Hall in the Back Bay. (Photograph by N.L. Stebbins; courtesy of Historic New England.)

Inside, classical forms give way to Rococo exuberance. Every surface is richly sculpted. Awestruck observers nicknamed it the "House of Gold," for the liberal use of gold leaf. Originally, thousands of bulbs outlined the edge of the balconies and the arches above the box seats. The lamps were covered over by the mid-1950s, when the house was demoted to a cinema. (Photograph by Will Rapport; courtesy of Harvard Theatre Collection.)

Galen's creative use of electric light was novel for its time. Note how the recessed fixtures blend seamlessly with the decor. The play of light and shadow gives greater depth to the walls and seems to intensify the drama onstage. The Majestic was the first theater to exploit electricity in this way, a feature that movie palaces would later pick up and perfect. (Photograph by Will Rapport; courtesy of Harvard Theatre Collection.)

The Majestic was also praised for its impeccable acoustics. The auditorium is shaped like an inverted bowl so that sound carries both out and up from the stage. The bare bulb at center stage is probably a ghost light, traditionally lit whenever the theater is dark. The exact origins of the superstition are murky, beyond the obvious safety factor. Some say the lamp wards away ghosts; others claim that it appeases them. (Photograph by Will Rapport; courtesy of Harvard Theatre Collection.)

Theatergoers squeeze through the narrow lobby of the Majestic, paying no attention to the decoration surrounding them. A richly ornamented entablature, thick with cherubs, greeted audiences in high style in the fall of 1954. In 1956, the Shubert-owned theater was sold to the Sack movie chain, along with the Plymouth, and renamed the Saxon. (Photograph by Will Rapport; courtesy of Harvard Theatre Collection.)

Chickering & Sons was once a world-renowned piano maker with deep roots on Piano Row. High-end instruments trickled into its Tremont Street showrooms from a factory in the South End. Two earlier warehouses, also on Tremont, had recital halls for society musicales. The shop next door advertises perforated music rolls for player pianos around 1912. (Courtesy of Boston Public Library.)

A different Chickering, Elmer, ran a prosperous West Street studio specializing in celebrity portraits that were sold at theaters as souvenirs. In 1903, he and his "flash specialist" Thomas C. Eustis outfitted a wagon as a portable studio and produced over 30 panoramic streetscapes of Boston. In this photograph, the two blocks of Piano Row frame the southeast corner of Boston Common. (Courtesy of Library of Congress.)

M. Steinert & Sons still operates the oldest retail music store in the country from its flagship showroom at 162 Boylston Street, the firm's home since 1896. A recital hall constructed in the bowels of the building became a mecca for classical musicians who nicknamed it the "Little Gem." (Courtesy of M. Steinert & Sons.)

Schoolchildren attend a concert at Steinert Hall, looking thoroughly unamused. Insulated from the street noise overhead, the elliptical hall is an acoustic marvel. It is also a fire trap. After a blaze ripped through the nearby Cocoanut Grove nightclub, city officials tightened fire codes, and the venue was abandoned. (Courtesy of Harvard Theatre Collection.)

Time and the elements have taken their toll on the forgotten hall, which once hosted concerts by violinist Fritz Kreisler and piano greats Ignacy Paderewski and Sergei Rachmaninoff. The 650-seat jewel was prized as an intimate setting for chamber music and vocal recitals. The low stage placed audiences near the action. The space is currently used for storage and as a piano graveyard. Leaks are inevitable 35 feet below ground, and a persistent damp is causing paint to peel and plaster

to crumble. Six panels, three on each wall, still bear the names of famous composers. Over the years, the buried hall's existence grew into something of an urban legend, and public interest in its rehabilitation has surged of late. This recent photograph, taken from the mezzanine, shows the slumbering hall in all its faded splendor. (Courtesy of Zach Pagano.)

Pedestrians cross Boylston Street at the Hotel Touraine on a blustery spring day in 1948. Banners advertising feature films, like the one spanning Tremont Street in the background, were a common sight in those days. The Majestic sports a new vertical sign. (Photograph by Leslie Jones; courtesy of Boston Public Library.)

Boylston Place, pictured around 1910, links Boston Common with the theater district. Three brick rowhouses at numbers 4, 5, and 6 have quartered the Tavern Club since 1887. Members still keep up the tradition of producing their own private theatricals in a theater on the second floor. An arch by Dimitri Gerakaris decorated with bronze lyres, pianos, and a whimsical bear in evening clothes—the Tavern Club's mascot—now marks the entrance to this urbane corner of Piano Row. (Courtesy of Revolutionary Spaces.)

Three

From Museums to Movie Palaces

The first theaters in Boston were manned by stock companies, with actors capable of playing a range of dramatic roles. In those early days, the lead usually went to a visiting—often English—star, as tastes in theater and the arts generally were imported from across the pond. The most celebrated of these companies took up residence at the shrewdly named Boston Museum in 1846, where they entertained, or rather enlightened, audiences. When the museum folded 50 years later, there were still those who stubbornly refused to believe they had stepped foot in a theater.

As stock companies died out, their mantle was taken up by an enterprising showman named B.F. Keith. Keith arrived penniless on Washington Street in 1882, intent on making a name for himself. From a makeshift theater above his dime museum, he presented a hodgepodge of acts with mainstream appeal: magicians, acrobats, comedians, trained animals, jugglers, singers, and dancers. Seemingly overnight, Keith and his partner, E.F. Albee, built a nationwide network of theaters that elevated the variety show into a mainstay of American popular culture. Their flagship theater, named after Keith, opened in 1894. The curtain rose at 10:00 a.m. and fell at 11:00 p.m. Audiences could come and go as they pleased, making vaudeville a cheap and wholesome way to kill time.

Film and vaudeville made a winning formula at first. A ticket to a stage show often included a short feature. But as films grew in length and quality, the balance shifted, and projection booths won out in most, though not all, of the district's playhouses. Newly built theaters, like the Modern and Paramount, were erected exclusively for film, with room enough onstage for an organ and little else. Meanwhile, legitimate theater came to be dominated by touring shows and Broadway bookings. And the once-booming district slowly began to contract.

Fine art was exhibited alongside curiosities at the Boston Museum from 1841 until 1846. It catered to all classes but was instantly popular among those who shunned the theater. A gallery on the top floor doubled as a "music saloon" for concerts and eventually plays. The museum quickly outgrew its porticoed home at the corner of Bromfield and Tremont Streets and relocated north of King's Chapel. (Courtesy of Boston Public Library.)

The new building transformed Moses Kimball's museum into a first-rate attraction. Contemporary accounts linger on the elegant iron balconies and the rows of glass globes glowing in the night "like enormous pearls." A rooftop observatory promised panoramic views of the city and harbor. Meanwhile, the collection continued to grow both in size and stature, adding Egyptian mummies and a waxworks to its catalog of curios. (Courtesy of Harvard Theatre Collection.)

The Great Hall lent credibility to even the most suspect exhibits, including a half-monkey/half-fish, which Kimball and his business partner, P.T. Barnum, puffed as a mermaid. If advertisements can be believed, the galleries contained over half a million artifacts. At 25¢, and with no extra charge for admission to the theater, it was billed as the cheapest entertainment in the world. (Photograph by N.L. Stebbins; courtesy of Harvard Theatre Collection.)

The Boston Museum was not the first museum to produce plays, but it was the first to make them respectable. Temperance and slavery dramas like *The Drunkard* and *Uncle Tom's Cabin* were favorites on the "lecture room" stage. In later years, the museum was known nationally for its stock acting company and for regular appearances by stage royalty like Edwin Booth, his brother John Wilkes, Mary Ann Vincent, and William Warren. (Photograph by N.L. Stebbins; courtesy of Boston Public Library.)

Gilbert and Sullivan's *H.M.S. Pinafore* was the first show to take the nation by storm. It premiered in 1878 on the stage of the Boston Museum, igniting what newspapers called *Pinafore* mania. For months, its popularity tested the theater's capacity. And before the year was out, an estimated 150 unauthorized productions were crisscrossing the country. Back in Boston, where the craze began, several pirated *Pinafores* were running simultaneously, none of which paid the authors any royalties. At right is one final look at the Boston Museum before it was demolished in 1903. A storefront sign reads, "Building Coming Down. Removal Sale." (Both, photograph by N.L. Stebbins; courtesy of Harvard Theatre Collection.)

Boston native Charlotte Cushman (left) became America's first theater celebrity abroad. Though conventionally unattractive, she had a commanding contralto voice that she used to great effect in breeches roles like Hamlet and Romeo—sometimes opposite her sister Susan's Juliet. This 1850s daguerreotype shows Cushman posing alongside her partner, Matilda Hayes, in matching tailored jackets. (Photograph by John H. Fitzgibbon; courtesy of Harvard Theatre Collection.)

Charlotte Cushman died in 1876 in her third-floor apartment at the Parker House (center), the same suite occupied by Charles Dickens in 1867–1868 during his second American tour. Cushman had made her debut two doors down at Tremont Temple. The Parker House is the oldest continuously operating hotel in the country, pictured here around 1900. (Photograph by T.E. Marr; courtesy of Boston Public Library.)

Boston has had three Tremont Theatres. The second and shortest-lived opened a block away from Tremont Temple in February 1863. It failed to gain traction under the management of Jane English and reverted to Allston Hall two years later. Sometime after that, it was made into a showroom for carpets. (Photograph by H.F. Holland; courtesy of Harvard Theatre Collection.)

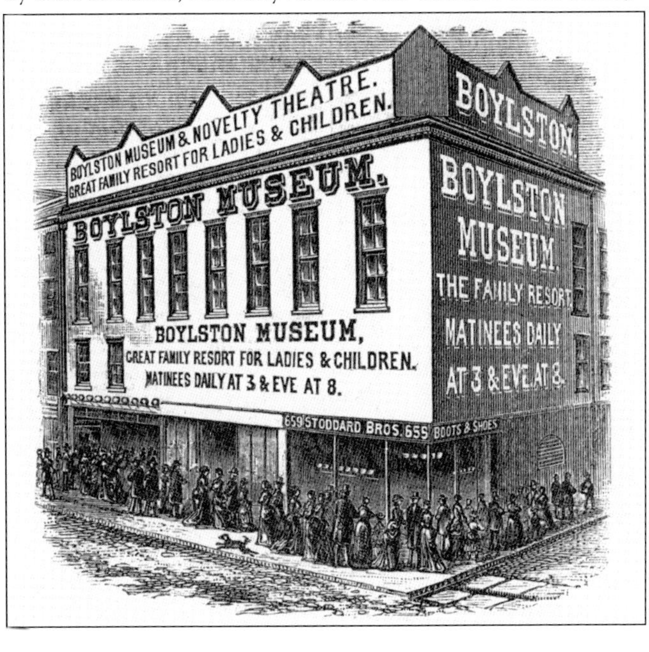

Following the lessons of the Boston Museum, dime museums instituted long hours and a family-friendly atmosphere. Their collections, of sometimes dubious authenticity, were meant to amuse more than edify. The Boylston Museum annexed a theater in 1876. An aquarium and menagerie were added to its next incarnation as the World's Museum. (Courtesy of Harvard Theatre Collection.)

News of President Garfield's assassination shut down theaters for days in September 1881. The Boston Theatre draped its entrance in mourning crepe, and a sign posted by manager Eugene Tompkins notified patrons that all amusements would be canceled until further notice. (Photograph by N.L. Stebbins; courtesy of Harvard Theatre Collection.)

Horticultural Hall replaced the old Boston Museum building in 1865. The lofty upper floors were reserved for exhibitions but were occasionally rented out for concerts. In 1882, the society leased the ground-level shops to a dime museum. Three years later, a traveling Japanese village took over the entire white granite structure while Gilbert and Sullivan's *Mikado* played at the nearby Hollis Street Theatre. (Courtesy of Boston Public Library.)

From its coveted seat on Tremont Row in Scollay Square, Austin & Stone's offered stiff competition to the waning Boston Museum. Labyrinthine halls were overfilled with the weird and wonderful: skeleton men, sword swallowers, tattooed ladies, and a poker-playing goat. An automaton named Adjeeb bested all who challenged him at checkers for 10¢ extra. This detail from an 1893 playbill shows the crush of streetcars converging at the museum's doorstep. (Courtesy of Harvard Theatre Collection.)

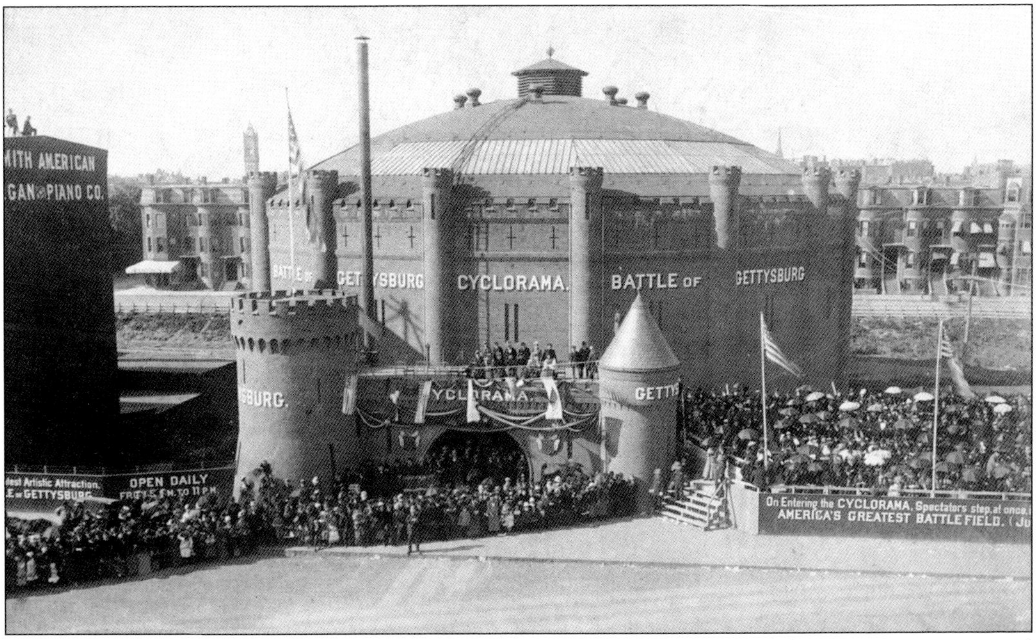

Some blockbuster entertainments simply outgrew the district. In 1884, a cyclorama was constructed in the South End to display a panoramic painting of the Battle of Gettysburg, 400 hundred feet long and 50 feet high. The cavernous rotunda was capped by one of the largest domes in the country, second only to the US Capitol. (Courtesy of Boston Public Library.)

Buildings often doubled as billboards. In 1895, the abandoned Tremont House hotel, which once stood opposite the Parker House, was papered over with posters promoting the engagement of Joseph Haworth at the Castle Square Theatre. The billposter seized the opportunity to plug his own services as well. (Courtesy of City of Boston Archives.)

The General Crane House was also rented out to advertisers before being demolished. The Colonial-era structure, located near the Hollis Street Theatre, had been the home of a Tea Party participant and Revolutionary War hero. The Shubert Theatre now stands in its stead. (Courtesy of Boston Public Library.)

The Castle Square Theatre was in the South End, several blocks from the district's epicenter. Between 1897 and 1903, the resident company presented an astounding 212 different plays across 3,700 performances. That averages out to 12 shows a week year-round, with a new play every 10 days. (Courtesy of Boston Public Library.)

The stock company dissolved in the 1920s. The Castle Square Theatre and the 500-room hotel that shared the building became early casualties of the Depression. The theater's razing in January 1933 exposed the skeleton of an old cyclorama that formed the shell of the auditorium. (Photograph by Leslie Jones; courtesy of Boston Public Library.)

Like the Howard Athenaeum, the Hollis Street Theatre started out as a church. In 1885, the arch windows of the old nave were bricked up, and the outer walls became the shell of a spacious 1,684-seat auditorium with standing room for 700. (Photograph by Arthur C. Haskell; courtesy of Library of Congress.)

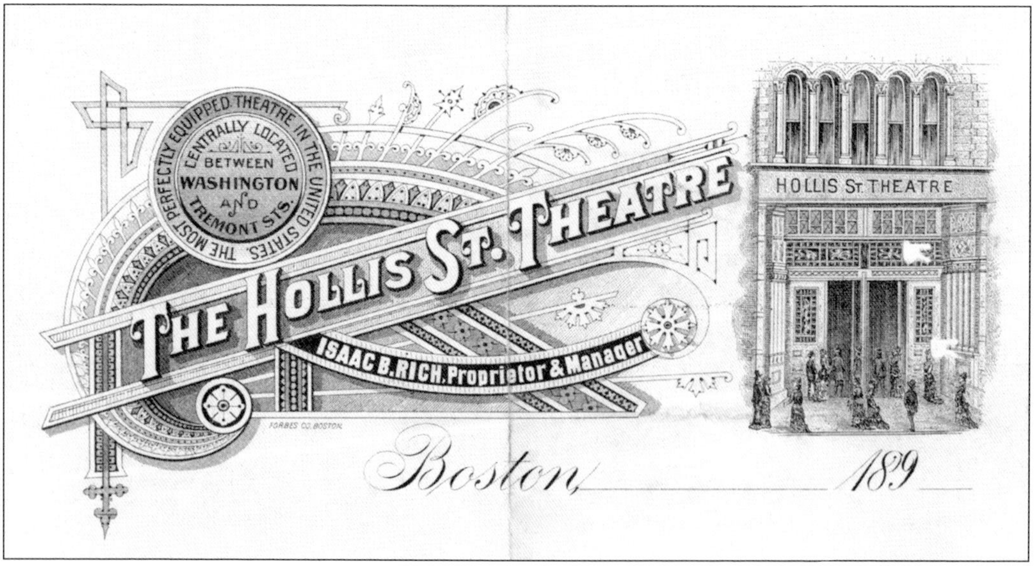
THE MOST PERFECTLY EQUIPPED THEATRE IN THE UNITED STATES.
CENTRALLY LOCATED BETWEEN WASHINGTON AND TREMONT STS.
THE HOLLIS ST. THEATRE
ISAAC B. RICH. Proprietor & Manager
HOLLIS ST. THEATRE
FORBES CO. BOSTON.
Boston, 189

A written "order" on this scrap of letterhead entitled its bearer to a seat at the fashionable Hollis Street Theatre in the 1890s. Note the flag-shaped punches. Comp tickets were usually issued by house staff to VIPs or the press or used to fill out the theater on slow nights, known in the biz as "papering the house." (Courtesy of Harvard Theatre Collection.)

This shot offers a peek into the green room at the Hollis Street Theatre. The comfortable lounge has been stripped of its finery. But theater memorabilia still line the walls, including signed photographs of past performers Maude Adams and Julia Marlowe. The stairs on the left lead up to the dressing rooms. (Photograph by Arthur C. Haskell; courtesy of Library of Congress.)

This photograph was taken around 1869 from the corner of Tremont and Hollis Streets. Tremont Street was widened twice over the next 50 years as theaters came to dominate the area, and this sparsely settled stretch became the main artery between downtown and the South End. The Shubert Theatre now occupies the lot on the left, joined by the Wang across the street. The Majestic and Wilbur Theatres were built farther up the block near Boston Common. (Courtesy of Boston Public Library.)

Twin taverns, the Lion and the Lamb, operated side by side on Washington Street in the early 1800s. The Lamb had long been a pickup point for the Providence stagecoach. It was succeeded by the Adams House hotel, the tall Victorian edifice on the left, around the same time that the Lion, next door, became an amphitheater. In 1884, the newly renovated Bijou Theatre occupied the second floor. Cue the arrival of B.F. Keith and the transformation of this street into the most storied block in all theatrical Boston. Keith, an ex–circus barker, opened a dime museum beneath the Bijou in 1884. Within a year, he had wrested control of the theater. There, he pioneered a mash-up of high and lowbrow amusements that revolutionized the industry and inaugurated a new form of mass entertainment: vaudeville. For the next 90 years, the former Lion site held as many as three simultaneously operating theaters—all run by Keith. The second Boston Theatre is just out of view to the north. (Photograph by Charles Pollock; courtesy of Boston Public Library.)

This nearly identical view was taken 20 years later, in 1906. After B.F. Keith took over the Bijou, he built his own playhouse directly behind it. O'Callaghan's storefront is below the old Bijou, sandwiched between the half-moon entrance to Keith's New Theatre and the Boston Theatre on the right. Keith's New Theatre became the seat of the sprawling Keith-Albee vaudeville empire, which controlled 400 theaters across the country. A bill posted outside Keith's Theatre presents a typical high-low lineup: the Fadettes, an all-female orchestra, followed by aerial acrobats the Four Lukens. Meanwhile, the Boston Theatre continued to present "legitimate" drama. The poster outside advertises Sarah Bernhardt's 1905 American tour—the first of four farewell tours to stop in Boston. (Courtesy of Library of Congress.)

The generator room powering Keith's showplace was described in *B.F. Keith's New Theatre, Boston, Mass*, as a noiseless "wonder shop of marble and swiftly-moving steel." Ever a showman, Keith installed a raised walkway with rails along the perimeter to allow visitors a look behind the scenes. Boston theater historian Donald King recalls seeing the room years later, long after the plant's dynamos were donated as scrap metal for the war effort. (Photograph by N.L. Stebbins; courtesy of Historic New England.)

Keith spared no expense, not even in the theater's mechanical underbelly. The switchboard was made of marble and its fixtures were nickel-plated. Fresh flowers were brought in daily, despite being 32 feet below ground and near a battery of coal-fired boilers. The potted palm appears to be healthy. (Courtesy of Harvard Theatre Collection.)

The Bijou reopened as the Bijou Dream in 1908. The movie house showed silent films accompanied by Keith's all-women orchestra. The most memorable features were the escalator, one of the first in Boston, and a crystal staircase, which had a lighted waterfall cascading underneath it. Four of the Bijou's exits led into adjacent theaters—the primary reason for its demolition. (Courtesy of Harvard Theatre Collection.)

In 1917, Harry Houdini escaped from a straitjacket while dangling upside down 100 feet in the air from Keith's Theatre. The publicity stunt, meant to drum up paying audiences, was witnessed by Sarah Bernhardt. During their first meeting a few days later, the 72-year-old actress reportedly asked if Houdini could use his magic powers to restore her amputated leg. (Courtesy of Harvard Theatre Collection.)

Houdini was a frequent performer on Keith's circuit. For eight weeks straight, the "Handcuff King" packed Keith's Theatre with the promise of a new feat at every appearance. At a matinee on February 11, 1907, he tantalized audiences with a handcuff escape while bound and nailed to a door. He returned that evening to accept a challenge from the employees of the Riverside Boiler Works, daring him to escape from an iron tank, which they proceeded to weld shut with Houdini chained inside. When he emerged 55 minutes later, "pale, weak, and trembling," in the words of John F. Kasson in *Houdini, Tarzan, and the Perfect Man*, "his face . . . bloody and his hands bruised," the audience leapt to their feet, their cheers deafening. Six men inspected the tank and found the rivets still in place. This photograph was taken on Houdini Night, March 2, 1906, and circulated in Keith's weekly newsletter with the caption: "Houdini jammed the great house to overflowing, with thousands still on the streets unable to press in." For once, it was not hyperbole. Along the walls of the theater, the standing room crowd numbered five people deep. (Photograph by N.L. Stebbins; courtesy of Harvard Theatre Collection.)

Sailors smile for the camera outside the Boston Theatre as they wait for the doors to open in December 1918. Boston's War Camp Community Service, a forerunner of the United Service Organizations, sponsored free shows for troops during World War I. The Bijou sign hangs overhead. (Courtesy of Schlesinger Library, Radcliffe Institute.)

Civilians watch from across the street as the line snakes past three Keith-operated theaters (from left to right): B.F. Keith's Theatre, the Bijou Dream, and the Boston Theatre. The line reportedly stretched for seven blocks. Bostonians were hard up for entertainment in late 1918, having rebounded from the flu pandemic that darkened theaters for weeks in the fall. (Courtesy of Schlesinger Library, Radcliffe Institute.)

Thousands of Army and Navy boys packed the house every Sunday afternoon. The 70-year-old Boston Theatre was beginning to show its age. As modern movie theaters sprung up on every corner, the steep, triple-tier balcony proved increasingly unfit for showing films. (Courtesy of Schlesinger Library, Radcliffe Institute.)

Keith and Albee established a foothold on Boston Common in time for the opening of the Tremont Street subway. Patrons could now enter Keith's Theatre through a walkway known as the Crystal Tunnel without stepping foot on Washington Street. In 1901, the five-story annex was plastered with advertisements promising continuous, high-class vaudeville and footage of President McKinley's second inauguration from the Biograph Company. (Courtesy of Harvard Theatre Collection.)

The Crystal Tunnel passed under Mason Street and fed directly into the auditorium. The walls and ceiling were covered with plate-glass mirrors and intricate plasterwork that ran the entire length of the passage. The tunnel was long abandoned by 1970 and had steam pipes running through it. (Photograph by C. John MacFarlane; courtesy of Library of Congress.)

By 1908, Keith's Tremont Street exterior had grown more ostentatious. Stained-glass windows lit up the night like a jeweled lantern. The Boston Theatre installed its own entry next door, prompting Keith to buy out his longtime competitor the next year. On the right of this postcard view sits Charles W. Hearn's portrait studio, where actors often went to be photographed. (Courtesy of Harvard Theatre Collection.)

The entrance to the Crystal Tunnel was later brutalized by a giant blade sign, shown here during Boston's tercentenary celebrations in 1930. Even after the Shubert Organization took over the lease to Keith's Theatre and renamed it the Apollo, the enormous eyesore remained in place. Alas, not even the Shuberts could make the old playhouse profitable. They tried changing its name again, this time to the Lyric. Still no one came. The market for vaudeville was thinning. By 1938, the Tremont Street entrance was being used exclusively for the Keith Memorial Theatre. In a few more years, the entire facade would vanish. (Left, courtesy of Library of Congress; below, courtesy of City of Boston Archives.)

Demolition commenced on the second Boston Theatre in the spring of 1926. An adjacent fire station, conveniently located against the theater's north wall, was torn down with it, giving the Keith Memorial Theatre room to expand. Soon afterward, a bogus headline in the *New York Times* proclaimed that a "mystery house" had been discovered within the theater's walls, dating to its construction in 1854. The structure turned out to be part of a sealed-off lobby, long since forgotten. Pictured above is a branch of the grand spiral staircase that led to the dress circle and up to the galleries. (Both, photograph by Leslie Jones; courtesy of Boston Public Library.)

The day after theatergoers bid a fond farewell to the Boston Theatre, its successor opened at the corner of Washington and Essex Streets. It was designed by the prominent theater architect Thomas Lamb as a temporary base while the Keith Memorial Theatre was under construction. It had everything audiences had come to expect from a Keith-Albee palace and more, including the city's first smoking room for women. (Courtesy of Harvard Theatre Collection.)

A million people thronged Boston Common in July 1927 to welcome back Charles Lindbergh from his transatlantic flight. Hoping to cash in, the Boston Theatre doled out these souvenir postcards with a doctored image of "Lindy" in the mirrored lobby. Fox Movietone's newsreel of Lindbergh's takeoff was the first popular sensation of sound film. Audiences filled local theaters to watch his plane roar down the runway. (Courtesy of Harvard Theatre Collection.)

The lavishly appointed B.F. Keith Memorial Theatre opened in 1928 with a star-studded gala. George M. Cohan, Lew Fields, Joe Weber, Fred Stone, Maggie Cline, Al Jolson, and Julia Arthur were all in attendance. The program lasted until after midnight. Before departing, members of the audience were treated to a hastily processed film of themselves gathering outside the theater. E.F. Albee supervised every detail of the monument to his longtime friend and business partner. Architect Thomas Lamb designed the soaring domed auditorium, which was decorated like a gilt and velvet jewel box. (Photograph by C. John MacFarlane; courtesy of Library of Congress.)

The outer lobby of the Keith Memorial Theatre was and still is a sight to behold. Patrons entering from Washington Street were met with an overawing display of marble, crystal, and brass. Its monumental columns were made of solid Italian marble rather than painted pilasters, a common shortcut in theaters. Straight ahead, an arcade of shops linked the lobby to the Crystal Tunnel and Tremont Street. (Courtesy of Library of Congress.)

Thickly carpeted stairs lead up from the grand lobby to a marble niche, where a spotlighted bust of B.F. Keith sits enshrined. Overhead, murals and chandeliers create a cocoon of baroque splendor and summon what one contemporary called "a dazzling architectural dream in ivory and gold." (Photograph by C. John MacFarlane; courtesy of Library of Congress.)

What was planned as a memorial to B.F. Keith turned out to be a memorial to vaudeville as well. At the theater's opening in 1928, feature films were presented alongside live vaudeville. But within a year, the stage shows depicted on this early program cover were dropped, and the theater became a dedicated movie house. (Courtesy of Harvard Theatre Collection.)

Even the mezzanine promenade, which served as an intermission lounge for balcony patrons, offered an unrivaled degree of luxury. It was said that the whole house felt more like a hotel than a theater. It contained a gymnasium, handball court, billiard room, nursery, laundry, kitchen, barbershop, and beauty parlor. Back-of-house accommodations were just as extravagant, with private bathrooms and showers for actors. (Photograph by C. John MacFarlane; courtesy of Library of Congress.)

The lack of bathrooms in Boston's earliest theaters kept many women at home. The Keith Memorial Theatre, on the other hand, was built with two opulent parlors for women. Adjoining powder rooms were outfitted with vanities so that ladies could freshen up in semi-privacy. Smoking in the ladies' lounge was "positively" prohibited, whereas men had their own lounge for that very purpose. (Courtesy of Harvard Theatre Collection.)

Scollay Square's Palace Theatre, built in 1891, joined the nearby Star, Olympia, Bowdoin, and Beacon Theatres in presenting small-time vaudeville and motion pictures. In 1894, the Palace Theatre introduced the first electric spotlight in the country, the same as those used on Navy warships. Previously, heated cylinders of mineral lime were used to produce an intensely bright beam for spotlighting, hence the term "limelight." In 1876, Alexander Graham Bell had carried out experiments in the fifth-floor garret at 109 Court Street. There he made the first telephone call, received three miles away in Somerville. (Courtesy of Library of Congress.)

The Star Theatre's peculiar facade was painted green and lit up by thousands of red and white bulbs. Behind the archway, a domed vestibule was strewn with more lights and set off with gold leaf, which dazzled by night. Here, a banner beckons passersby to a silent Western, *The Hold-Up in Buckeye Canyon*. Next door, Austin & Stone's awaits the wrecking ball. The Olympia Theatre took its place in 1913. (Courtesy of Revolutionary Spaces.)

The Star Theatre's nearest rival stood a stone's throw away. Constructed in 1906, the Theatre Comique was the first purpose-built movie house in Boston. Within a year, the Unique, Lyric, Premier, and Joliette Theatres opened in swift succession—all 10¢ nickelodeons. A typical program ran half an hour and included a short film and "illustrated songs" that changed weekly. (Courtesy of Revolutionary Spaces.)

In 1913, Clarence Blackall turned two Victorian storefronts into the most dignified cinema in Boston. Thanks to an exclusive contract with Warner Bros., the Modern Theatre had dibs on new releases like the 1926 blockbuster advertised here. *The Sea Beast*, starring John Barrymore, was the first film adaptation of *Moby-Dick*. The Modern was renamed the Mayflower in 1949 and served a stint as a porno movie house in the 1970s. (Courtesy of John Toto.)

With its classical front and plush interior, the Modern Theatre may look anything but modern. The real innovations were invisible. Wallace Clement Sabine, a Harvard physicist and pioneering acoustician, consulted on sound, which in the silent film era came from a console organ in front of the stage. In 1928, the cozy 800-seat auditorium was retrofitted with speakers for Boston's first talkie, *The Jazz Singer.* (Courtesy of John Toto.)

Theater mogul Jacob Lourie introduced back-to-back films at the Modern and Beacon Theatres in an effort to compete with the larger vaudeville houses. The double feature fast became an industry standard. To cut costs, Lourie began offering the same bill at both theaters. Their close proximity made it easy to swap reels by streetcar between showings. (Courtesy of Boston Public Library.)

The spotlight first trained on Lotta Crabtree in the goldfields of California. Before long, "Little Lotta" was touring the nation with her own company. Audiences everywhere adored her. She was a maverick, an ageless ingenue who smoked cigars and wore trousers. She retired to Boston at age 45 and died a millionaire in 1924, the city's second-largest taxpayer. The bulk of her estate she left in a charitable trust for the care of veterans, ex-convicts, aging actors, and animals. She purchased the Park Theatre and constructed a tunnel from the theater to her private residence at the Brewster Hotel, which she also owned. Below, a film crew shoots a scene outside the Park Theatre on Washington Street in 1909. (Left, photograph by J. Gurney & Son, courtesy of Library of Congress; below, courtesy of Harvard Library.)

In a sobering photograph from 1909, two young girls sent to gather firewood to heat their home struggle under the load. On the other side of Washington Street, in the distance, is a rare glimpse of the Unique Theatre (later renamed Stuart), which operated as a nickelodeon; the Globe Theatre stands behind it. Both buildings survive, though not as theaters. (Photograph by Lewis Hine; courtesy of Library of Congress.)

Bowdoin Square Theatre was dwarfed by the Art Deco headquarters of the New England Telephone and Telegraph Company in 1934. The rival Palace Theatre once stood straight ahead, amid the tangle of streets that met at Scollay Square. The Custom House Tower was completed in 1915, becoming New England's tallest skyscraper. (Courtesy of Harvard Theatre Collection.)

Today, Winter Street is closed to traffic, preserving a measure of pedestrian charm. But before World War I, the side street was bustling. In those days, the intersection of Summer, Winter, and Washington Streets, pictured here in the distance, was Boston's busiest corner. The Orpheum marquee marks the entrance to Winter Place and the revered Boston Music Hall. (Courtesy of Harvard Theatre Collection.)

Shoppers lured downtown by department stores like Filene's, Gilchrist's, and Jordan Marsh dodge traffic near the heart of the retail district in 1932. Many made a day of it, catching a matinee or evening show. To the north stood Newspaper Row, the nerve center of the *Globe*, *Herald*, *Journal*, *Post*, and other dailies. (Photograph by Leslie Jones; courtesy of Boston Public Library.)

The Music Hall still lives on as the Orpheum. In 1910, it was altered beyond recognition by movie magnate Marcus Loew. Like Keith, he added an entrance to siphon off some of the heavy foot traffic on Washington Street. This photograph looks south toward the Modern Theatre, past a traffic kiosk that was operated manually from the middle of the street. While some streetcar traffic had gone underground, the junction at Winter and Washington Streets was still causing headaches. From 1975 to 1979, the Orpheum served as the unlikely base of the Opera Company of Boston. The stage was only 26 feet deep, much too shallow for opera, and there was no orchestra pit. Several rows of seats had to be removed to make room for the players. Nowadays, the mixed-use hall retains the feel of an old-school movie house, though it is used primarily for live music concerts. This entrance on Washington Street no longer exists. (Photograph by Roy J. Jacoby; courtesy of Boston Public Library.)

The Metropolitan Theatre was the last and by far the largest of Clarence Blackall's Boston theaters. The press exaggerated its size at 5,000 seats; the true count was closer to 4,400. What mattered was that Boston finally had a movie house of palatial proportions, one befitting its name. The Met was one of vaudeville's last citadels until 1938, when stage shows were replaced by a steady diet of first-run films. (Courtesy of Harvard Theatre Collection.)

Workmen prepare for the Met's debut in 1925, perched atop ladders to reach the nymphs reclining on the auditorium's colossal portals. The Met was then, as now, one of the largest theaters in the world. Its stage can accommodate the largest touring opera and ballet companies. It was returned to its prime in the late 1980s and rechristened the Wang. Like most renovated theaters, it seats fewer people today. (Courtesy of Harvard Theatre Collection.)

By the 1930s, Boston's Broadway was ablaze with electric light. In this photograph, the clock at White's department store has just struck 7:00 p.m. The crowds usually swarming the sidewalk are settling into their seats, hushed and expectant. The street, too, has fallen silent. One can sense the excitement as the curtain rises. There was plenty to do after the show as well. Double features were playing at the Modern with new films every week. (Photograph by Arthur Griffin; courtesy of Griffin Museum of Photography.)

Behind the glitz and glamour, theaters were struggling to stay afloat. Attendance plummeted in the first years of the Depression. After the repeal of Prohibition, Keith's Theatre rebranded as the Normandie ballroom, pictured here in the winter of 1935. The orchestra was cleared for a dance floor, and the lengthy lobby turned into a bar. It reverted to a movie house in 1939 as fortunes improved. (Photograph by Arthur Hansen; courtesy of Revolutionary Spaces.)

Workmen clear the site of Keith's Theatre in 1952. Onlookers line Mason Street, an alley at the stage end of the theater, to inspect the rubble. Keith's had gone by a dizzying number of names over its downhill career: Apollo, Lyric, Normandie, Art Movie, and Mirth Movie. Its final act as the Laffmovie Theatre made it a favorite haunt for children and teenagers. (Photograph by Leslie Jones; courtesy of Boston Public Library.)

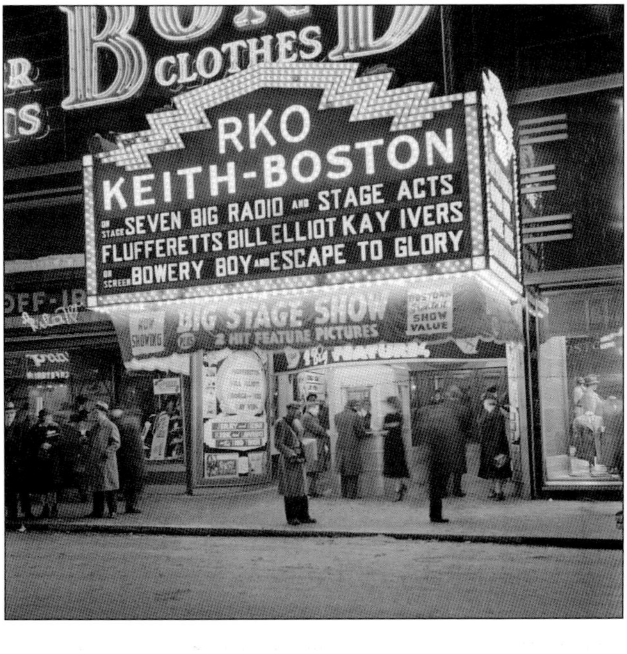

The Boston Theatre carried on as a "vaude-filmer" until the 1940s. Keith's circuit merged with rival Orpheum and became part of RKO Pictures in 1928, hence the new name. The auditorium is still intact, though long disused. The entryway is gone and instead leads down to the Chinatown subway station. (Photograph by Richard Merrill; courtesy of Boston Public Library.)

Built in 1932 on the foundation of the Adams House, the Paramount Theatre was the last of Boston's big-time cinemas. It was designed exclusively for films, a sure sign that times were changing. The magnificent Art Moderne marquee, with a ribbon of neon reaching skyward, is still Washington Street's most iconic landmark. The sign features a glittering array of 7,000 lights, which float up in flashing champagne bubbles. The Hotel Avery, pictured here in the 1950s, was another building by Clarence Blackall. In its twilight years, it was rented out to performers and theater folk. Soda bars and cafeterias enlivened the strip by day, while cocktail lounges and nightclubs kept the area hopping after hours. (Photograph by Nishan Bichajian; courtesy of MIT Libraries.)

Four

BROADWAY OR BUST

There is an old adage in the theater that plays are not written, they are rewritten. For much of the 20th century, that rewriting took place on Tremont Street over two-week stints known as tryouts. These trial runs gave playgoers the chance to see first drafts of darling musicals and daring new dramas on the road to Broadway. More importantly, tryouts gave directors the chance to cut, tweak, polish, and perfect a show in front of a crowd every bit as discerning as their New York counterparts. Richard Rodgers, of Rodgers and Hammerstein fame, used to say that he would not open a can of tomatoes without first bringing it to Boston.

Anecdotes abound of runaway hits and first-night flops. Tennessee Williams's first professionally produced play, *Battle of Angels*, met with such hostility that a planned Broadway engagement was canceled. It did not help that onstage pyrotechnics caused a panic in the theater on opening night. When *The King and I* opened a few songs shy of a classic, Oscar Hammerstein penned new lyrics for a discarded melody from *South Pacific*. The recycled tune, *Getting to Know You*, became a Broadway standard. And in 1965, Neil Simon revised the third act of *The Odd Couple* on the advice of Boston drama critic Elliot Norton. Simon and others later credited Norton with rescuing at least half a dozen shows from crash landing on the Great White Way.

The tryout system petered out in the 1970s as more producers substituted previews in New York for expensive runs out-of-town. Boston's clout as a theater town largely went with it. Audiences dwindled, and theaters turned to proven, post-Broadway fare in order to attract them. In 2019, the Ambassador Theatre Group took charge of the Emerson Colonial Theatre and reopened the old Broadway beacon with the world premiere of *Moulin Rouge! The Musical*. One of their ambitions, the group says, is reestablishing the Colonial's legacy as a birthplace of Broadway hits.

Elliot Norton scoffed at the notion that his reviews could make or break a play. He preferred instead to "doctor." His column, which printed nearly 6,000 reviews for shows he often saw twice—at either end of their Boston run—was required reading for Broadway producers. Playwrights would often pick his brain while in town and publicly credited Norton with turning tryouts into triumphs. (Courtesy of Harvard Theatre Collection.)

When *Our Town* debuted at the Wilbur Theatre in 1938, a New York press agent painted it as a flop: "The American Athens wanted no truck with a play without scenery," he wrote. "To Beacon Hill Brahmins, such an omission was as confusing as tackling a grapefruit without a spoon." *Our Town* retreated from Boston after a single week but went on to win the Pulitzer Prize anyway. (Photograph by Vandamm Studio; courtesy of Harvard Theatre Collection.)

Cole Porter (second from right) poses for publicity shots with Betty Grable, Bert Lahr, and Ethel Merman on the set of his Broadway-bound musical *Du Barry Was a Lady* at the Shubert in 1939. Merman had previously starred in Porter's *Anything Goes*, which gave its first road performance a block away at the Colonial. (Photograph by George Karger; courtesy of the LIFE Images Collection via Getty Images.)

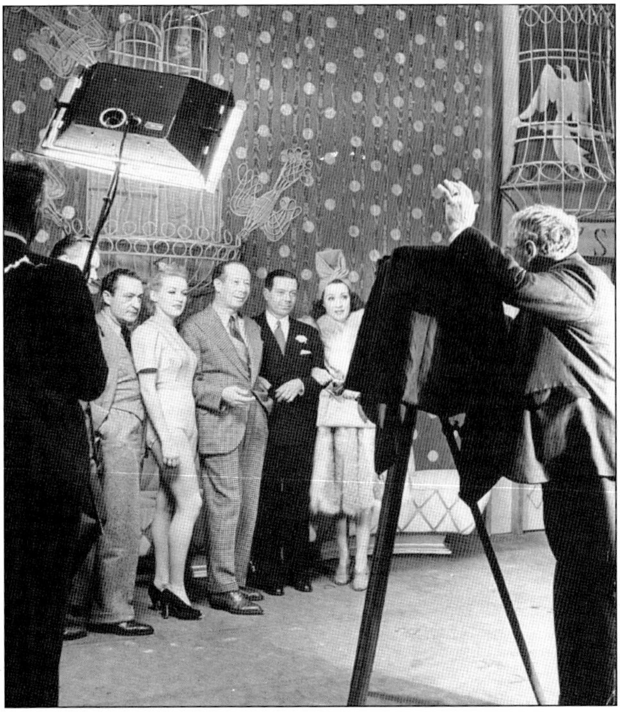

Fans pose with vaudevillian Jimmy Durante outside the Plymouth Theatre in January 1939. Emaline Mechanic (second from left) was active in local theater productions and an avid playgoer. This photograph is taken from an album she compiled of autographed snapshots. Many show her with the leading performers of the day, including John Barrymore, Bob Hope, Helen Hayes, and Tallulah Bankhead. (Courtesy of Harvard Theatre Collection.)

This shot of actress-singer Ella Logan was taken by the same fan at the stage door of the Shubert Theatre in 1939. Logan was starring in the final installment of George White's *Scandals*, a long-running musical revue modeled after the *Ziegfeld Follies*. (Photograph by Emaline Mechanic; courtesy of Harvard Theatre Collection.)

The Shubert Organization owned and operated seven Boston stages, including three at the heart of the theater district, pictured here in 1930. The Wilbur is on the left. The Majestic and Shubert Theatres are on the right. The Shubert monopoly actually preserved the district through the lean years of the Depression. In 1956, antitrust legislation caused the organization to sell off all its Boston holdings except its namesake theater. (Courtesy of Revolutionary Spaces.)

The world premiere in 1935 of *Porgy and Bess* at the Colonial featured the largest all-black cast ever to perform on an American stage. The cast of classically trained singers appear on the set for Catfish Row designed by Serge Soudeikine. (Photograph by Vandamm Studio; courtesy of Harvard Theatre Collection.)

Composer George Gershwin takes a curtain call during a 15-minute ovation on opening night, September 30, 1935. At left stand director and producer Rouben Mamoulian, Anne Brown as Bess, and Todd Duncan as Porgy. Gershwin continued to refine the music throughout the show's one-week run. (Courtesy of Harvard Theatre Collection.)

Paul Robeson starred as the first black Othello in a major production of Shakespeare's play in the United States. A two-week engagement ran at the Brattle Theatre in Cambridge in 1942 before transferring to the Colonial and then to Broadway, where it ran for a record-smashing 296 performances. The production then embarked on a lengthy and culturally daring national tour. Robeson was an uncompromising activist who refused to be bullied into an "inferior brand" of freedom, even though his views often left him professionally ostracized. "I'm looking for freedom," he declared years later, "*full freedom*." As a testament to his fame and bargaining clout, Robeson's contract with the Theatre Guild denied to any segregated venue the pleasure of his smoldering performance. As a result, the tour never stopped in the South, where Jim Crow laws were still enforced. Robeson's *Othello* remains the longest-running production of a Shakespeare play in Broadway history. (Courtesy of Harvard Theatre Collection.)

Away We Go! was slow going when it reached Boston in March 1943. The show sorely needed a rousing number. A second-act duet was rescored for chorus, becoming an instant showstopper and lending its name to the stately musical. *Oklahoma!* opened on Broadway to rave reviews, but not in time for the new title to appear on the printed sheet music. (Courtesy of Harvard Theatre Collection.)

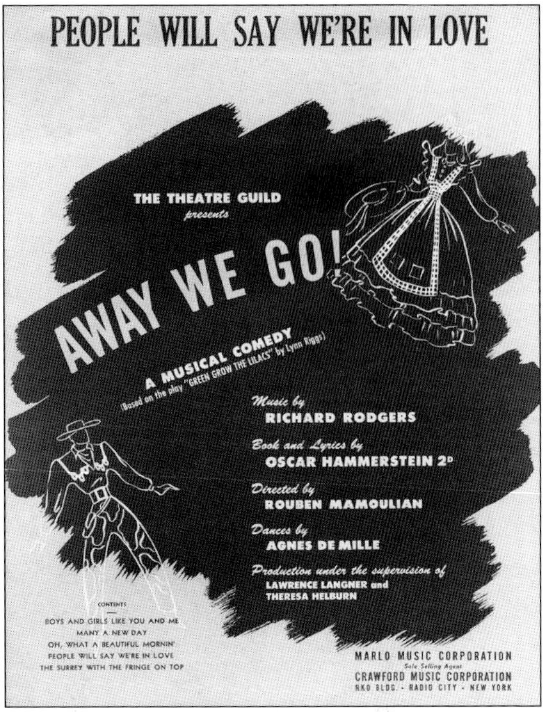

Richard Rodgers and Oscar Hammerstein II read reviews in the Public Garden during tryouts for *Allegro* in 1947. Local audiences dealt the famed songwriters their first commercial failure after a string of hits with *Oklahoma!* and *Carousel*, both of which were workshopped at the Colonial Theatre. (Courtesy of Rodgers and Hammerstein: A Concord Company.)

Broadway chronicler Al Hirschfeld made regular trips to Boston, sketchbook in hand. Most of his drawings were published in the *New York Times* ahead of a Broadway opening or alongside a review. Here, he depicts Gertrude Lawrence and Yul Brynner during a preview of *The King and I* at the Shubert in 1951. Next to his signature he has written "Boston." (© The Al Hirschfeld Foundation. www.AlHirschfeldFoundation.org.)

A 1926 widening of Tremont Street cost the Shubert its original entryway and part of its lobby. Over the years, the theater has welcomed a stream of celebrity imports, some for their very first appearances in America: Julie Andrews and Richard Burton in *Camelot*, John Gielgud in *Hamlet*, Angela Lansbury in *Gypsy*, and Laurence Olivier playing a washed-up comic in *The Entertainer*. (Photograph by Will Rapport; courtesy of Harvard Theatre Collection.)

Jacqueline Kennedy flew in from the family compound on Cape Cod to attend a performance of *Sail Away* during tryouts at the Colonial Theatre in 1961. Playwright Noël Coward escorted her through the lobby, buffered from the adoring crowd by a police escort and the First Lady's Secret Service detail. (Courtesy of Harvard Theatre Collection.)

Creative teams met frequently in the carpeted ladies' lounge of the Colonial Theatre to iron out a show. At one such meeting, choreographer Bob Fosse leapt atop the onyx table at left to improvise a tap routine for *Dancin'*, accidentally chipping it. The scar has become a good luck charm for visiting artists ever since. (Photograph by Patrick Farrell; courtesy of Emerson Colonial Theatre, an Ambassador Theatre Group venue.)

The 1978–1979 season brought new plays to Boston, including *Tribute*, starring Jack Lemmon, and touring productions of *A Chorus Line*, *Annie*, and *The Wiz*, an all-black retelling of L. Frank Baum's *The Wonderful Wizard of Oz*. (Used by Permission. All rights reserved, Playbill Inc; courtesy of Harvard Theatre Collection.)

Fans brave the cold for the season's hottest ticket. A touring production of *A Chorus Line* opened at the Shubert in December 1977 while still running strong on Broadway. The hit musical returned three more times over the next six years. The outgoing production, *For Colored Girls Who Have Considered Suicide / When the Rainbow Is Enuf*, was the city's first chance to see the trailblazing work of Ntozake Shange. (Photograph by George Rizer; courtesy of the *Boston Globe* via Getty Images.)

Five

BANNED IN BOSTON

Long after the 1750 crackdown on public performances, Boston enjoyed a reputation for being a killjoy. Performers on B.F. Keith's circuit coined the term "Boston version" to refer to the sanitized rendition of a vaudeville routine. Early attempts at policing the stage were carried out by the Watch and Ward Society, an unmerry band of moral crusaders made up largely of ministers and Boston Brahmins. Their cause gained the force of law in the early 20th century when the city established a three-man board of censors.

In 1960, Richard J. Sinnott assumed the post of chief of the Licensing Division. The aptness of his name, sin-not, was not lost on anyone. Like his predecessors, Sinnott declared open season on immorality. The most powerful weapon at his disposal was three infamous words, "Banned in Boston." With them came the power to revoke a theater's license, amend scripts, or block shows outright. The ban's effect proved to be a two-edged sword, however. "I would rather be banned in Boston than read anywhere else," Upton Sinclair said famously. "Because when you are banned in Boston, you are read everywhere else." The same logic applied to the stage, where the seal of disapproval provided the box office bump many shows were looking for. When the producers of a scantily clad ballet could not convince Sinnott to ban their production, they sent him a cheeky note of thanks after it closed early in New York. The position of city censor was eliminated in 1982. By then, its powers were considerably weakened by a series of Supreme Court rulings, including one involving the Boston production of *Hair*.

In Scollay Square, burlesque queens danced on more or less with impunity. Sly means were devised for ducking the vice squads. At the Old Howard, a blinking light in the footlight trough alerted dancers to their arrival, and clothes would miraculously materialize. After Scollay Square was plowed under, city officials set aside a 5.5-acre playground for vice in 1974. That zoning is technically still on the books.

While African Americans were not banned from Boston theaters, they were not welcomed either. In 1853, Sarah Parker Remond and her two companions were denied seats in the dress circle at the Howard Athenaeum. When Remond refused to move to the segregated gallery, a confrontation broke out. She was roughed up by a guard and forcibly ejected from the theater. She later sued for damages and won. Remond was no stranger to discrimination. In the 1830s, she and her two siblings were expelled from a Salem high school after white parents protested the presence of black children. Remond would go on to become a sought-after lecturer for the American Anti-Slavery Society and a physician. Massachusetts did not outlaw segregation in public spaces, including theaters, until after the Civil War. (Courtesy of Peabody Essex Museum.)

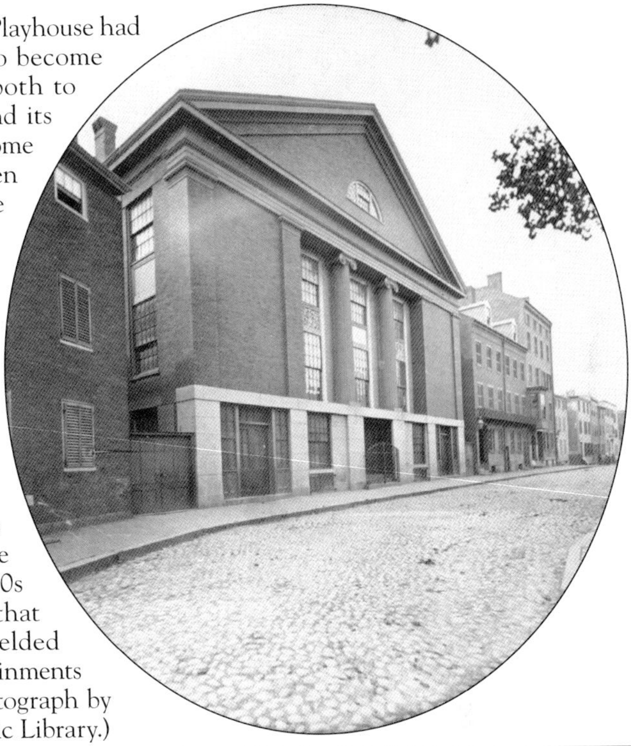

Elliot Norton joked that the Charles Playhouse had "the proper sinned-in atmosphere to become a great theater." He was referring both to its checkered past as a speakeasy and its saintlier origins. Built in 1839, it was home to a Universalist congregation and then to Boston's first synagogue. In 1958, the Actors Company of Boston turned it into a hotspot of the regional theater movement. (Photograph by Josiah Johnson Hawes; courtesy of Boston Public Library.)

Scollay Square was a pleasure seeker's paradise. This 1912 photograph shows Tremont Row overgrown with signage. Beneath the Scollay Square marquee is the Rialto (formerly the Star), Boston's only all-night movie house. The entire square was swallowed up in the 1960s by a massive urban renewal project that transformed the West End and yielded Government Center. The adult entertainments migrated to the Combat Zone. (Photograph by Leslie Jones; courtesy of Boston Public Library.)

At the Old Howard, vaudeville and variety gave over to bump and grind striptease. The vice squad stepped up raids in the 1930s and 1940s, urged on by the blue-nosed Watch and Ward Society. Still, business was brisk, and the Old Howard became known, among other things, for rounding out the education of Harvard undergrads and their professors. (Courtesy of Revolutionary Spaces.)

Burlesque queen Ann Corio relaxes in her dressing room at the Old Howard. When asked why burlesque had become a spectator sport for so many women, Corio replied wryly, "This is nothing new. If Salome had had one veil instead of seven, John the Baptist might be alive today." Her popularity among women prompted the theater to install a ladies' restroom. (Photograph by Leslie Jones; courtesy of Boston Public Library.)

Corio's supporting dancers sashay in crop tops for a spread in the Sunday *Boston Globe*. The racy image, shown here with original crop marks, featured another quip from Corio: "You know I can't sing . . . but the audience doesn't seem to mind." (Courtesy of Harvard Theatre Collection.)

This shot was taken from the gallery during a rare lull in the action. Usually the Old Howard lived up to its motto, "Always something doing." Some of the more infamous doings involved would-be politicians like John F. Kennedy. In 1953, the lively palace of peel was finally shuttered on charges of indecency. (Photograph by Will Rapport; courtesy of Harvard Theatre Collection.)

Theaters settled cheek by jowl along this claustrophobic stretch of lower Washington Street. On the right, swarms of people descend on the Stuart, Globe, Olympia, and Boston Theatres. In 1928, the area was well on its way to earning the sobriquet "Gay Times Square." A number of dance halls and dive bars enriched its nightlife. Some, like the Petty Lounge and Touraine Café, provided a safe haven for gays and other "improper" Bostonians who cruised the district. The Stuart Theatre, in particular, was known for its permissiveness. Around the corner, Playland Café began attracting gay clientele by the start of World War II. It was known affectionately as an "upholstered sewer." The area changed dramatically when sleazy venues overran the neighborhood in the 1960s. The blocks between Essex and Kneeland Streets were officially zoned for adult entertainment in 1974 in an effort to contain the spread. (Courtesy of the History Project: Documenting LGBTQ Boston.)

This photograph looks back in the opposite direction, capturing the pulse-quickening pace at street level. A single horse carriage can be seen amid the scramble of motorcars. The Olympia and Globe Theatres are visible in the background. In 50 years, this area would become ground zero for X-rated businesses. (Courtesy of Revolutionary Spaces.)

Lewis Hine documented the plight of child laborers in the early 20th century. But in this 1909 photograph, captioned "The Beginning of the Theatre Habit," he turned his lens on leisure. Children attending the theater was not the only issue on reform agendas. Hine's employer, the National Child Labor Committee, had campaigned for years to curtail appearances by child performers on big-time circuits like Keith's. (Courtesy of Library of Congress.)

Elvira Johnson performed at the Gaiety Theatre alongside scores of black entertainers, including Jazz Age icons Josephine Baker, Florence Mills, and Ethel Waters. In the Roaring Twenties, the Gaiety was one of only two venues in the city to offer racially integrated acts to integrated audiences. The Casino in Scollay Square was the other. (Photograph by Apeda Studio; courtesy of Harvard Theatre Collection.)

The third Globe to grace Washington Street was built for vaudeville by comedy duo Weber and Fields in 1903, after designs by city architect Arthur H. Vinal. Today, a Chinese grocery occupies the ground floor. The former mezzanine, now a dim sum restaurant, retains much of the original decor. (Courtesy of City of Boston Archives.)

When burlesque took over, the Globe began offering midnight shows, except on Saturdays of course. Movies replaced live shows on Sundays, when "glorified" burlesque proved too risqué for city censors. Live shows started up again at 12:01 a.m. sharp on Monday. Note the men in uniform, frequent patrons of burlesque halls in Scollay Square and on lower Washington Street. The sidewalk box office was clearly a later addition, as was the glittering marquee. (Photograph by Three Lions; courtesy of Getty Images.)

Bawdy burlesque gave way to film in the 1950s, and the Globe became the Center Theatre. The movie house changed hands again in the 1970s and screened Chinese-language films as the Pagoda until 1995. Across the street, the Publix followed suit. To an earlier generation, it was known as the Gaiety. (Photograph by Nishan Bichajian; courtesy of MIT Libraries.)

Moviegoers huddle beneath the glowing marquee at RKO Keith's during a March snowstorm. The sleeper hit of 1943 was a lurid exposé of the Hitler Youth titled *Hitler's Children*. As with plays, the city censor screened every new picture and issued cuts. They also issued a set of additional cuts for Sunday showings. (Photograph by Richard Merrill; courtesy of Boston Public Library.)

Margaret Webster directs a rehearsal of *Othello* at the Colonial Theatre in 1942. Two years earlier, an ill-fated production of Tennessee Williams's play *Battle of Angels* had tested her reputation after literally going up in smoke. On opening night, flash pots set to go off in the final scene sent clouds of smoke billowing over the footlights. Pandemonium ensued as the audience bolted for the exits. (Courtesy of Harvard Theatre Collection.)

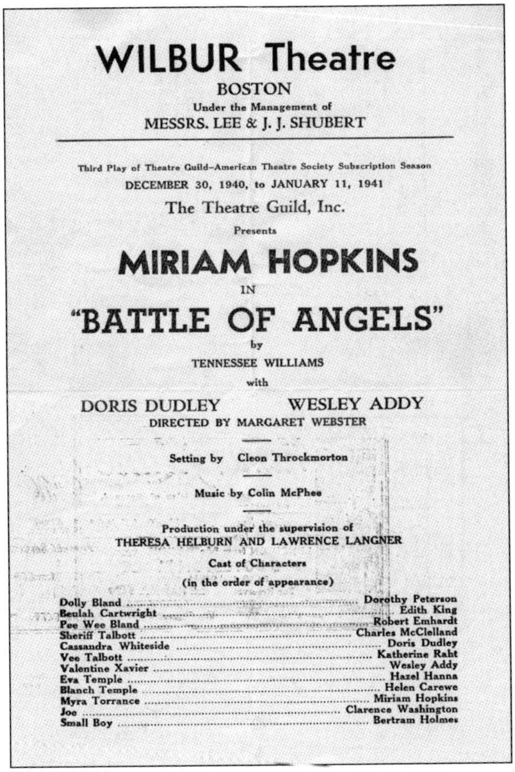

WILBUR Theatre
BOSTON
Under the Management of
MESSRS. LEE & J. J. SHUBERT

Third Play of Theatre Guild–American Theatre Society Subscription Season
DECEMBER 30, 1940, to JANUARY 11, 1941
The Theatre Guild, Inc.
Presents
MIRIAM HOPKINS
IN
"BATTLE OF ANGELS"
by
TENNESSEE WILLIAMS
with
DORIS DUDLEY WESLEY ADDY
DIRECTED BY MARGARET WEBSTER

Setting by Cleon Throckmorton

Music by Colin McPhee

Production under the supervision of
THERESA HELBURN AND LAWRENCE LANGNER

Cast of Characters
(in the order of appearance)

Dolly Bland .... Dorothy Peterson
Beulah Cartwright .... Edith King
Pee Wee Bland .... Robert Emhardt
Sheriff Talbott .... Charles McClelland
Cassandra Whiteside .... Doris Dudley
Vee Talbott .... Katherine Raht
Valentine Xavier .... Wesley Addy
Eva Temple .... Hazel Hanna
Blanch Temple .... Helen Carewe
Myra Torrance .... Miriam Hopkins
Joe .... Clarence Washington
Small Boy .... Bertram Holmes

Battle of Angels fell prey to puritanical Boston censors, who objected to its violent and sexual themes. Tennessee Williams called them "prissy old maids." The play's star, Miriam Hopkins, rose to the playwright's defense: "Miriam Hopkins says Boston Council should be thrown in harbor with tea," headlined one local newspaper after she held a press conference to rescue the production. (Courtesy of Harvard Theatre Collection.)

The Theatre Guild had intended to bring *Battle of Angels* to Broadway. Playbills, like this one, for the run at the National Theatre in New York had already been printed and subscriptions sold. But the company abruptly canceled the engagement. Humiliated, Tennessee Williams took to referring to the defeat in his diary as "A.B."—after Boston. (Courtesy of Harvard Theatre Collection.)

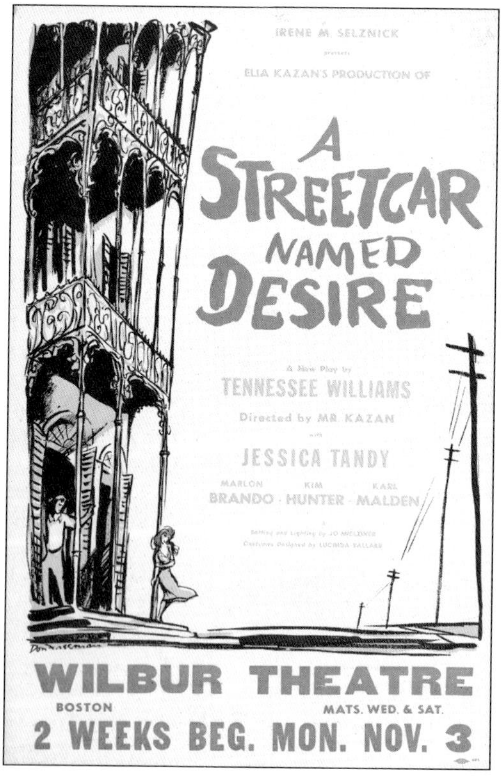

A Streetcar Named Desire met with mostly positive reviews in 1947, despite outcries over the rape of Blanche DuBois, which was acted from behind a screen at the censor's behest. In a letter home from Boston, Tennessee Williams warned his own mother against coming. "Some reviewers [are] a bit shocked by the play . . . Really think you should wait . . . as this play is hardly your dish." (Courtesy of Harvard Theatre Collection.)

Before arriving in Boston in 1970, *Hair* had played in over 14 US cities. But Boston was the first to legally challenge the "tribal love-rock musical." The district attorney threatened to arrest the producers and the cast, shown here in rehearsal at the Wilbur Theatre, for violating the state's obscenity laws. The city censor agreed with him. "I had the misfortune of viewing the worst collection of garbage I've ever seen on a Boston theater stage," he cried, adding, "Anyone who abuses the flag should be horsewhipped in public on Boston Common." As the case went to court, the *Boston Globe* came out in favor of the musical and ran an editorial headed, "'*Hair*' is how you view it," along with a three-column cartoon showing a justice sneaking off with a nude bust of Venus. (Courtesy of Harvard Theatre Collection.)

Hair cut short its run on April 10, 1970, rather than comply with changes to the notorious nude scene as ordered by the state supreme court. That night, members of the cast performed from the balcony of the Wilbur Theatre to the crowd gathered below. A subsequent ruling overturned the decision and was upheld by the US Supreme Court. The show reopened six weeks later, uncut and uncensored. (Courtesy of Harvard Theatre Collection.)

Tickets sold for up to $10 a pop and advance sales topped $800,000. This ticket was never used because it was for the same night *Hair* closed in protest. The cast draped the front of the Wilbur in funeral black, but mercifully for Sinnott there was no flag burning. (Courtesy of Harvard Theatre Collection.)

A Vietnam veteran marches past the State Theatre (formerly the Park) during an antiwar demonstration in April 1971. The Combat Zone got its name from the many sailors on shore leave who frequented the strip clubs and brothels while in uniform, and because high crime rates left it looking like a war zone. (Photograph by Jeff Albertson; courtesy of UMass Amherst Libraries.)

A flyer advertises a showing of *One-Armed Swordsman*, an early kung fu flick by Chang Che, at the National Theatre in 1971. Chinatown merchants used to rent the State Theatre on Friday and Monday nights. Instead of the usual adult fare, they showed movies from Hong Kong as a cheap diversion for the community. (Photograph by Gil Friedberg; courtesy of the *Boston Globe* via Getty Images.)

Strip clubs lined either side of Washington Street with names like the Teddy Bare Lounge, Pussycat, and the Naked i Cabaret. David Waller, a former Parker House doorman, salvaged the iconic 30-foot marquee after the Naked i Cabaret closed on New Year's Eve in 1995. It is currently on display at West End Johnnie's in Boston along with memorabilia from the Old Howard. The neon sign's most salacious feature—a blinking eye superimposed on upturned legs—remains in storage, too vivid a reminder of the vanished world of sex and squalor. The Naked i Cabaret was leveled for a parking lot in 1996. (Courtesy of Spencer Grant.)

The Pilgrim made national headlines in 1974 after Congressman Wilbur Mills received an onstage kiss from a stripper named Fanne Foxe. Mills insisted that they were merely friends, but his act proved to be a political showstopper. This 1912 image, from the city's censorship files, shows the former Olympia's distinctive archway—a trait shared by its sister theater in Scollay Square. Neither building survives. (Courtesy of City of Boston Archives.)

The Combat Zone was largely snuffed out in the 1990s, following a crackdown on prostitution. The closing of its seedy cinemas had more to do with the advent of the VCR than the tactics of the oft-maligned Boston Redevelopment Authority. Two strip clubs remain: Centerfolds and the Glass Slipper, both on LaGrange Street. (Courtesy of the Estate of Jerry Berndt.)

Six

STAGING A COMEBACK

"If the history of the Theater District is ever written," Mayor Thomas Menino declared in 2007, "Emerson College should be the first five chapters." With apologies to the mayor, this is chapter six. But it is time to talk about Emerson College and its role in the rebirth of Boston's downtown theaters. Its decision to relocate from Back Bay to the theater district in the 1990s has been a leading factor in its miraculous turnaround.

A spate of efforts to reclaim the rundown rialto had been underway for several years but picked up steam in 1995. That year, the National Trust for Historic Preservation singled out the Boston Opera House and the neighboring Paramount and Modern Theatres as one of the 11 most endangered sites in the country. Mayor Menino moved to halt the demolition of other playhouses on Washington Street. And in 2004, a major overhaul of the Boston Opera House was the first sign that the tide was changing.

In 2009, Emerson transformed the crumbling Paramount Theatre into a multi-venue arts center before embarking on an ambitious rehabilitation of the Majestic. The fate of the Colonial, Emerson's third historic property, remained unclear. Plans to convert the auditorium into a cafeteria were scrapped after a public outcry reached the ears of Broadway legend Stephen Sondheim, whose groundbreaking musicals *Follies* and *A Little Night Music* previewed there in the 1970s. Emerson reversed course and recommitted to bringing the city's oldest continuously operating theater back from the brink. The Emerson Colonial Theatre reopened in 2018 following a multimillion-dollar revitalization by the London-based Ambassador Theatre Group, which is leasing the space from Emerson for 40 years.

The bright lights of Washington Street beckon once again, transporting audiences back to the district's glory days. The resurrected houses, which include the Suffolk University–owned Modern Theatre, rank among the most cherished landmarks in Boston and have inspired a wider renaissance on Washington Street. To those who recall the sleaze and sin of the Combat Zone with a mixture of fear and curiosity, the area is almost unrecognizable.

The third National Theatre towers over Tremont Street in 1935. The old Cyclorama is on the left. The 1911 theater was swept away in the 1990s after weathering a century of urban change. The Cyclorama was saved and incorporated into a new visual and performing arts complex, the Boston Center for the Arts, south of the present-day theater district. (Courtesy of Revolutionary Spaces.)

Flyman Ed Lynn readies backstage for a performance of *The Nutcracker* by the Boston Ballet in 1980. Behind him is the manual counterweight system used to swap scenery at the Wang Theatre. An earlier form of stage rigging that relied on rope and sandbags was still in use at the Colonial until 2018, when it ceased to be a "hemp house." (Photograph by David L. Ryan; courtesy of the *Boston Globe* via Getty Images.)

The Plymouth marquee was dismantled ahead of its reopening as the Gary Cinema in 1958. Built in 1911 by Clarence Blackall, the theater was demolished in 1978 to make way for the mammoth State Transportation Building, seen at the time as a lifeline for the blighted neighborhood. Emerson College's Tufte Performance and Production Center now occupies a corner of the Plymouth's old footprint. It includes two stages and a host of media production studios that connect to the Majestic Theatre. (Photograph by Will Rapport; courtesy of Harvard Theatre Collection.)

This dreary streetscape shows the Modern Theatre languishing in sorry dilapidation. Its graceful archway has been boarded up. The Keith Memorial Theatre has not fared much better and looks strangely out of place amid dumped mattresses. Businesses retreated as crime spilled over into the district, turning it into a magnet for drug dealers, hoodlums, and pickpockets. (Photograph by David Prifti; courtesy of Boston Public Library.)

The Modern Theatre sat vacant for 30 years until Suffolk University announced plans to redevelop the property. The city agreed, on the condition that the 1914 facade was salvaged. In 2009, the marble and sandstone exterior was taken apart stone by stone, cataloged, cleaned, and reassembled at the head of a brand new state-of-the-art theater. A 10-story residence hall capped the new construction. (Courtesy of Boston Landmarks Commission.)

The Keith Memorial Theatre blossoms with terra-cotta ornament. After decades of neglect, the district's most flamboyant facade began to lose its luster. The Sack Theatre chain purchased the shabby showplace in 1965 and refurbished it. The original Lamb-designed marquee was removed and replaced with the one shown here. The new owner converted the dressing rooms into apartments. He also bricked up the proscenium arch and installed a second movie screen on the stage. The two theaters, Savoy 1 and 2, eked by for a few years, despite being outnumbered by porn palaces. Its closest neighbor, the Paramount, yielded in 1974, leaving the Savoy as the sole first-run movie house on Washington Street. Unable to turn a profit, Sack pulled out in 1978. (Courtesy of Boston Landmarks Commission.)

When Sack moved out, the Opera Company of Boston moved in. The Sack-era changes were reversed, and the brick wall enclosing the stage was torn down. In August 1979, the new occupants gleefully burned a copy of the theater's mortgage on the stage, surrounded by the set for *Madame Butterfly*. Thereafter, the Keith Memorial Theatre became the Boston Opera House. The company owned the theater outright, but the cost of maintaining it was staggering. Facing mounting debts, the company went bankrupt, and the house fell again into disrepair. It was finally restored in 2004, after years on the National Trust's Most Endangered Places list. Today, it sports a new corporate moniker, Citizens Bank Opera House, and is home to the Boston Ballet and a steady stream of touring Broadway shows. (Photograph by C. John MacFarlane; courtesy of Library of Congress.)

Four decades after going dark, the Paramount relit its dazzling Art Deco marquee. When the Paramount opened in 1932, it had a single screen with a stage that was only 10 feet deep. The new Emerson Paramount Center still includes a screening room, but its main stage was completely rebuilt to accommodate live performances. The intricate Art Deco interiors were restored as well and rank among the finest examples in the city. The exterior now looks strikingly close to this photograph, minus the mid-century automobile. (Photograph by Nishan Bichajian; courtesy of MIT Libraries.)

The new Paramount Center added a screening room, rehearsal studios, and a residence hall on the adjoining site. An LED wall, spelling out "Bijou," animates the darkened front of the arcade, the last vestige of the 1882 theater. Washington Street's other refurbished jewels include the Boston Opera House and the Modern Theatre, known together as the "Three Sisters." (Courtesy of Bruce T. Martin.)

A new tower, part of the Paramount Center expansion, pays tribute to the site's rich lineage. A long line of theaters have occupied the plot since 1836. The earliest was the Lion, followed by the Melodeon, Gaiety, and Bijou Theatres. B.F. Keith's namesake theater was its most famous tenant. (Courtesy of Phil Boucher.)

Rust has eaten away at the lettering over the door to the Gaiety Theatre. In 2005, the Friends of the Gaiety lost a valiant bid to save the historic burlesque house. Their cause was thwarted by a city report denying the theater landmark status. A window exhibit in the upscale apartment building that replaced the Gaiety reminds passersby what they missed: "You are standing at the doorway of three-dozen heart breakers. Only you're a century too late." (Photograph by George Rizer; courtesy of the *Boston Globe* via Getty Images.)

The Colonial's box office is hopping again. The counter was lowered to comply with new building codes, but ticket prices have soared. The original scale of prices from 1900 is on display. Tickets ranged from 50¢ for second balcony seats to $12 for orchestra boxes. (Photograph by Marc J. Franklin; courtesy of Emerson Colonial Theatre, an Ambassador Theatre Group venue.)

The Colonial's lobby is gilded to the gills, like its model at Versailles. In 2018, the entire house was painstakingly rehabbed. Crews spent more than 37,000 man-hours retouching gold leaf, repairing murals, recreating plaster molds, and installing some 42,000 square feet of carpet, custom ordered from the original manufacturer. The large plate-glass mirrors are original to the building. Below, the lobby's double helix staircase is an unusual feature for a theater. Like any spiral stair, it saves space. It also helps with crowd control. Patrons headed to and from the dress circle and balcony can do so without crossing paths. (Above, photograph by Marc J. Franklin; below, photograph by Patrick Farrell, courtesy of Emerson Colonial Theatre, an Ambassador Theatre Group venue.)

The Colonial's splendorous auditorium received a fresh coat of cerulean paint with a hand-stenciled overlay. The original color was discovered under decades-old crimson wallpaper. In 1900, Clarence Blackall oversaw every detail of the hall's design with an eye for comfort. Four slender columns supporting the balcony and gallery were deliberately placed in the rear of the orchestra to create unbroken sightlines. Years later, playwright Neil Simon was known to pace anxiously at the back of the house while audiences took in his work for the first time. The *Odd Couple* premiered here in 1965, followed by *Plaza Suite* in 1968, and *Promises, Promises* the following year. Two wall plaques were recently placed a few strides apart to honor the playwright's legacy and invite others to experience his "creative process." (Photograph by Patrick Farrell; courtesy of Emerson Colonial Theatre, an Ambassador Theatre Group venue.)

Boston's "House of Gold" reopened as the Emerson Cutler Majestic Theatre in time for its centenary in 2003. A gift from arts philanthropists Ted and Joan Cutler spurred the year-long renovation, which rolled back decades of deterioration and restored the venue to its former, glittering glory. Its round and lavish auditorium, which some have likened to an inside-out Faberge egg, is a marvel of artistry and engineering. A trellis of garlanded arches enfolds the auditorium in a welcoming embrace. Thanks to the cantilevered balconies—the first in a Boston theater—there is not a bad seat in the house. The best seats are in rows C and D of the center balcony, which are composed of original chairs from the orchestra section. (Courtesy of Bruce T. Martin.)

Discover Thousands of Local History Books Featuring Millions of Vintage Images

Arcadia Publishing, the leading local history publisher in the United States, is committed to making history accessible and meaningful through publishing books that celebrate and preserve the heritage of America's people and places.

Find more books like this at
www.arcadiapublishing.com

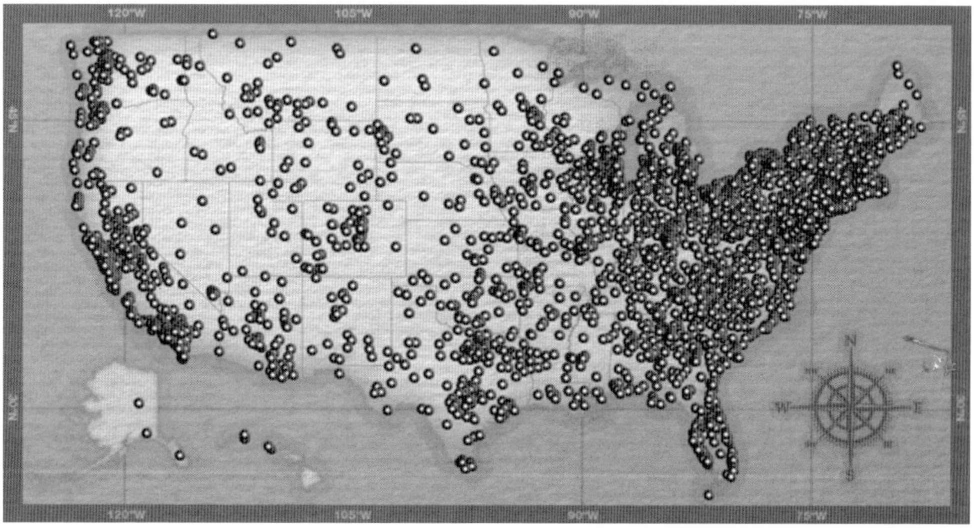

Search for your hometown history, your old stomping grounds, and even your favorite sports team.

Consistent with our mission to preserve history on a local level, this book was printed in South Carolina on American-made paper and manufactured entirely in the United States. Products carrying the accredited Forest Stewardship Council (FSC) label are printed on 100 percent FSC-certified paper.

MADE IN THE USA